Japan as I See It

装幀 ● 菊地信義
装画 ● 野村俊夫

翻訳 ● Don Kenny（ダン・ケニー）
イラスト ● 大森只光
写真資料提供 ● 神戸市立博物館
　　　　　　　倉橋町役場
DTPオペレーション ● ポイントライン

Published by Kodansha International Ltd.,
17-14, Otowa 1-chome, Bunkyo-ku, Tokyo 112-8652.

Copyright © 1997 NHK Overseas Broadcasting Department

First Edition 1997
ISBN 4-7700-2197-6

00 01 02 03　10 9 8 7 6

英語で話す「日本の文化」
Japan as I See It

NHK国際局文化プロジェクト［編］
ダン・ケニー［訳］

まえがき

　本書は、1985年に講談社から『私の日本文化論』シリーズとして出版された3冊、『日本のこころ』『日本文化を探る』『日本らしさ』から選んだ10篇です。

　『私の日本文化論』は、NHKの国際放送・ラジオ日本が、1982年に放送を始めた番組です。1回15分で、日本語を含む21言語で放送しました。

　世界中に日本製品があふれているのに、それを作る日本人の顔が見えてこないという、海外の声に応えて生まれた番組で、私はチーフプロデューサーを務めました。

　コンピューターのおかげで大量の情報が瞬時に得られる時代になりましたが、今あらためて読み返してみると、時の流れに押し流されることなく、深く、静かに、日本の文化を見据える眼が感じられます。

Preface

This book consists of ten essays selected from the *Japan as I See It* series (*Japanese Sensitivities, Behind Japanese Culture, and Japanese Essences*) published by Kodansha in 1985.

Radio Japan, an international broadcasting service of NHK, began producing *Japan as I See It* in 1982. Each segment was fifteen minutes long, and was broadcast in twenty-one different languages including Japanese.

The program was created in response to a call from overseas—although Japanese products were flooding markets around the world, many people felt the absence of a Japanese cultural presence behind the products. I served as the chief producer of the program.

The computer has recently made it possible for people around the world to access a huge volume of information instantaneously. Yet on reading these essays again I was struck by the penetrating eye the authors turned on Japanese culture—one that is not swayed by the currents of the times.

本書が、日本の文化について語り、あるいは、
考え直してみようとする人々の良き友になれるも
のと確信しています。

1997年9月

橋 本 定 久
昭和女子大学教授

I have no doubt that this book will serve as an excellent introduction—or reintroduction—to the essence of Japanese culture.

September, 1997

Sadahisa Hashimoto
Professor, Shōwa Women's University

目 次

Contents

日本語のこころ
The Heart of the Japanese Language

金田一春彦
Haruhiko Kindaichi

日本人が何気なく使う言葉は、外国人にはずいぶん奇異に響くことがあるようです。たとえば、道で思いがけなく知人に逢ったとします。日本人はその時によく、「どちらへいらっしゃいますか」とたずねます。外国人のうちには、「おれがどこへ行こうと勝手ではないか、おれの私生活に入ってくるな」といいたくなる人があるかもしれません。

日本人がそういう質問をするのは、「この人にきょう、思いがけないところで逢った。この人に何か変わったことでも起こったのではないか。それならば一緒に心配してあげよう」というやさしい気持からそういうのです。ですから聞かれた人は、簡単に、「ちょっとそこまで」といえばそれでよろしいのです。

Some of the things that Japanese people say to each other in the course of their daily lives sound very strange to foreigners. For instance, when we run into an acquaintance on the street, we often say, "Where are you going?" Foreigners may well want to answer such a question with "What difference does it make to you where I'm going? Stay out of my private life!"

A Japanese who asks such a question is expressing surprise at meeting his friend in such an unexpected place, inquiring as to whether or not something is wrong, and offering sympathy and concern. So all the other person has to say is, "Oh, I'm just going a little bit further on."

たずねた人は安心して、「ではどうぞお大事に」といって、それ以上聞こうとはしません。解放してくれます。そのような場合に、決して「子供の成績が悪いから学校へ呼び出されて行くんです」といったようなことを正直にいう必要は少しもありません。そんなことを答えたら、かえってたずねた人が困ってしまいます。

　日本人は、知り合いどうしは、お互いに、相手のことを心配しあおうという気持をもって生活しているのです。

　日本人はまた、はじめての人に、「お子さまは何人ですか」とたずねることがよくあります。相手が女の人の場合、「そういう質問をすることは、失礼ではないか」と、よく西洋人などは思う人がいるようであります。これもべつにその人の秘密を探ろうというわけで聞いているのではありません。

　日本人は、昔から家というものを大切に考えました。子供が生まれないで家の血統が絶えてしまっては大変だと思っておりました。ですからこのようなことを聞くのでありまして、答える方も大体正直にいっております。「3人です」というふうに答える。そうすると相手は、「それはご安心ですね」、あるいは、「それはお賑やかで結構ですね」といったようなことをいって喜んでくれます。

　1人しか子供がいない場合には、「まだ1人です」

When the person who asked the question hears this answer, he is relieved and says, "Well then, take care of yourself." And then the two part. In such a case, there is no need at all for the person being questioned to explain with such details as "My child's grades are so bad that I have been asked to go to his school and talk with his teacher." In fact, the questioner would feel very uncomfortable if you were to answer with such personal details.

Japanese people carry on their daily lives with feelings of concern for each other's welfare.

Japanese people also have the custom of asking someone they have just met how many children they have. It seems that foreign women sometimes feel this is an extremely rude question. But it is not an attempt to ferret out a person's secrets.

Since ancient times, the Japanese have considered home and family very important aspects of life. They believe that it would be a terrible thing if no children were born and the family line became extinct. This is the reason such questions are asked, and most Japanese answer them honestly. If one simply answers "Three children," the questioner will happily reply, "Oh, that's good," or "You must be very busy with them."

In the case of one child, the normal answer is "We still

と答えます。そうしますと、「それはお寂しいですね」といってみたり、あるいは、「もうお1人ぐらい（子供があった方がよろしいのに）」というようなことをいうと思います。これも、こちらの家というものを心配してくれている、そう考えて、日本人は子供のことを聞かれても、それをいやがりません。

　それから、日本人が知り合いの家を訪ねたといたします。その時に、よくおみやげを持って行きます。そのおみやげを差し出す時のあいさつが、また変わっております。「これはまことにつまらないものですが」といって差し出します。アメリカの人などは、はじめてこの言葉を聞きますと、「つまらないものを持ってこないで、もっといいものを持ってくればいいではないか」と思うようであります。

　ではなぜ日本人は、そのような場合に、「つまらないものを」というのでしょうか。日本人は、ほかの人から何か好意を受ける場合、そのことをいつまでも覚えていて、将来それに対して報いをしなければいけない、と思っております。日本人は、そういうことから、その前に何か好意を受けた場合、その次に逢った時にはそのことを必ず話題にします。そうして、「先日はありがとうございました」というようなお礼の言葉をのべます。もしそれを忘れておりますと、「恩知らず」といわれます。そうしてまた、お礼の言葉をのべるだ

have only one child," and the response is something like, "You must be very lonely," or "You should have at least one more." Japanese people understand that such questions arise from feelings of concern for their families, so they do not feel offended.

When Japanese people go to visit the home of an acquaintance, they frequently take a gift, and the greeting that is commonly made when offering such a gift is also strange to foreign ears. We say, "This is really an insignificant thing I offer you." When Americans hear these words for the first time, they often wonder why the visitor did not bring a more worthwhile gift.

Let us think about the reasons Japanese people say that their gift is insignificant. When someone does a Japanese person a favor, the recipient never forgets it and always feels as though he must do something to repay the kindness. Thus, he invariably mentions his gratitude the next time he meets the person who has done the favor for him with such words as "Thank you so much for your kindness the other day." If such a greeting is neglected, the person is thought to be extremely ungrateful and rude. Beyond this greeting, the recipient also strives to do something in return for the favor that is equal in value.

けではなくてその好意に相当するお返しをしよう
と思います。

こういう習慣がありますと、日本人は他人のと
ころに物をおみやげに持って行きにくくなりま
す。つまり相手に、「今度はおまえの方から持っ
てこい」と言っていることになってしまうからで
あります。そこで物を持って行く時には、「これ
はつまらないものだ。だからあなたは（私に）お
返しをしようとしないでもいいのだ」とこういわ
ないではいられない気持になります。
「つまらないものですが」というのは、そういう、
「これはお返しの心配は全然いらないものだ」と
いう言葉の代わりであります。

日本人はほかの人に何かご馳走する場合、「何
もございませんが、召し上がってください」とよ
く申します。もしほんとうに何もなかったら、食
べられるはずがありません。

これはどういうことかといいますと、「これを食
べても食べなかったと思ってください」という意
味でいっているのであります。ですから、「つま
らないものですが」といっているのとまったく同
じ精神であります。

さらに、日本人は、久しぶりで逢った人に対し
て、「先日は失礼いたしました」という人が多い
ようであります。これは、外国人のうちには、や
はり心配する人が多いようであります。「自分は
確かにこの前この人に逢った。その時には、この

With such customs prevailing, it is difficult for Japanese to take gifts to people, because it seems to indicate that something is expected in return in the future. Thus, they feel obliged to say that the gift they have brought is of no value, and therefore there is no need for the person to whom they are offering it to feel any future obligation.

Thus, the expression "This is really an insignificant thing I offer you," really means "There is no need at all for you to concern yourself with giving me anything in return."

When Japanese people serve their guests a meal they often say, "I have nothing at all to offer you, but please eat what there is." Of course, if there really was not anything to offer, the guests could not eat.

The meaning of this expression is "Even though you eat this, please do not feel that you have eaten anything." In other words, it comes from the same way of thinking as the phrase, "This is really an insignificant thing I offer you."

Further, when Japanese people meet someone they have not seen for some time, they often say "I was most rude the other day." This also seems to cause concern to a lot of foreigners, because it makes them think in the following manner—"I do indeed remember seeing this person the other

人は何も自分に悪いことはしなかった。それなのにいま、『先日は失礼しました』というところを見ると、自分の知らない間にこの人は私に何か悪いことをしたのかもしれない」そう考えて心配する人があるといいます。

　が、実際にはそのような心配をする必要は全然ありません。日本人はこう考えているのです。「私はこの前この人に逢った時に悪いことをした覚えはべつにない。しかし自分は不注意な人間だ。だから自分は悪いことをしたつもりはないけれども、この人に何か迷惑がかかるようなことをしたかもしれない。それならば、今あやまっておかなければ（いけない）」これが日本人が考えることであります。

　一般に日本人は、あやまる言葉をよく使います。お礼をいう代わりによくあやまる言葉を使います。

　たとえば、バスにおばあさんが乗ってきました。そうすると、坐っている人が立って席を譲ります。その時におばあさんは何というか。「ありがとうございます」とお礼の言葉をのべる人もあります。しかし、「すみません」といって、あやまる言葉を述べる人の方がはるかに多いようです。

　おばあさんの気持はこうなのです。「私が乗ってこなければ、あなたはいつまでもそこに坐っていられたでしょう。私が乗ってきたばかりにあなたがお立ちになるということで、あなたにご迷惑

day but I cannot remember him doing anything that seemed rude to me, so he must have done something rude that I didn't notice."

But there is actually no need at all to worry like this, because the Japanese person who says this is thinking in the following manner—"I do not remember doing anything particularly rude to this person when I saw him the other day, but since I am a careless person, I may have done something that was a bother to him without knowing it, so I must apologize for anything that I may have done."

Japanese people do indeed use a great number of words of apology. Very often, they use an apology in place of words of gratitude.

For instance, an old woman gets on a bus. Someone gets up to give her their seat. While there are some old ladies who will say a simple "Thank you," most people will say, "I'm sorry" in such a situation.

An old lady who says "I'm sorry" is thinking like this—"If I had not boarded this bus, you would have been able to keep your seat. Since you got up because I got on the bus, I have been a bother to you. I am indeed sorry for this." It is

をおかけする。これは申し訳ありません」という気持の表明であります。そういうことから、日本人は感謝の言葉をのべる代わりにあやまる言葉を述べる。その方がまた、聞く人は快いと感じます。

日本人は、一般に謝罪の言葉をのべることを大変尊びます。日本人の中で、西洋へ行って外国人のメイドさんを雇った人があります。

台所でコップがこわれました。メイドさんは、日本人の奥さんにこういったそうです。「コップがこわれました」これは、その国ではごく普通の言葉かもしれません。しかし日本人は、このようにいわれますとあまりいい気持ではありません。

日本人の場合はどういうか。「コップをこわしました」と、こういうのです。つまり、コップが割れたのは、自分の不注意のせいである。それは自分が力を加えてわざと割ったのと同じことである。自然にそのコップが割れたのとはちがうと、そう考えて、「コップをこわしました」といって謝罪の意味をあらわすわけです。これが日本人の場合、相手に大変快く響きます。

日本の警察では、同じく罪を犯した人に対して、あやまり方のよい人には、罰を軽くします。つまり、「あやまった人は、その罪を後悔している。もう悪いことは二度としないだろう」と考えて、罰を軽くいたします。

ところが近頃、自動車に乗る人の間に、「事故

for this reason that Japanese apologize instead of expressing direct gratitude. We feel that this approach makes people feel better than direct gratitude.

Japanese people generally feel that apologizing is an extremely honorable thing to do. The story is told of a Japanese family who went to live in a Western country. They hired a maid from that country.

She broke a glass in the kitchen and said to the wife of the family, "The glass broke." This may well be the normal way to report such a matter in Western society, but the Japanese wife did not like it when she was spoken to in this manner.

If the maid had been Japanese, she would have said, "I broke a glass." In other words, she would be saying that the breaking of the glass was the result of her own negligence. And to her it means the same thing as it would if she had broken it on purpose. She would never think that the glass just broke of its own accord. Thus, we would say, "I broke this glass," as an expression of apology. This sort of attitude is extremely effective in dealing with Japanese people.

Japanese police give a person who knows how to apologize well a much lighter punishment than one who does not. This is because the Japanese believe that a person who apologizes regrets having committed the crime and this also makes them confident that he will never do anything bad again.

But recently, drivers of automobiles have begun to feel that

を起こした時に警察に呼ばれてあやまると損をする。（あやまると）自分の罰を認めたことになる。だから、あくまでも自分は悪くないとがんばる方が得だ」と、そういった考えが広まりつつあります。これは、ヨーロッパ、アメリカあたりの影響ではないかと思いますけれども、私は、これは大変悲しいことだと思います。

　ところで、日本人は、あやまる場合に、ただ「すみません」といって頭を下げるそれだけの方がいい、弁解しない方がいいという考えがあります。それは、弁解するということは、自分は罪がないということを表わすからであります。口数はなるべく少なく、深く頭を下げて悔悛の情がおもてに出るということ、これが最上のあやまり方とされております。

　こういう考えの中には、日本人はあまり口数は多くない方がいいという考えが入っております。男は無駄口をきくものではないというふうにして日本の男の子は育てられます。

　かといって、公の席では、女の人が男の人をさしおいてしゃべるということは、なおよくないというふうに考えられてきました。実際昔から日本の女の人は、自分の意見はあっても、それは口にしないで目上の人のいうなりになるということが、最高の女性の徳というふうに考えられてきました。ですから上に立つ男の人は、女の人の気持を考えて振る舞わなければなりません。

it is not practical to apologize when they are called to the station for causing an accident. They believe that apologizing indicates that they are admitting they are at fault, and that they place themselves in a more advantageous position by insisting that they are innocent. I cannot help but feel that this has come from the influence of Europe and America, and I am greatly saddened to see this phenomenon arising among us.

When Japanese people apologize, they consider it best to simply bow their head and say, "I'm sorry," rather than adding any explanatory defense for what they have done, because they feel that any such defense means that you do not recognize that you are at fault. The best apology is expressed in the least possible number of words, with the head bowed as low as possible, and with a look of contrition on the face.

Generally speaking, the Japanese consider it best not to talk too much in any situation. Japanese boys are taught that a man should never speak any more than is absolutely necessary.

And they do not consider it proper for a woman to talk more than a man in public. Since ancient times it has been believed that a woman should never express herself verbally, but rather should always quietly carry out what she is told by her superiors. This is considered the highest feminine virtue. Thus, as the man is in a superior position, he must act in such a way that the woman's thoughts and feelings are taken into consideration.

こういった気持は、今でもいくらか伝わっております。いっしょに喫茶店やレストランに入ります。男が、「何を食べようか」と、こういいます。女は、「何でも」と、こういう。そうすると男は、この女は何が好きだろうかと考えて、（女が）好きそうなものを考えて注文する。それが望ましい男のやり方でありました。もっとも、なかにはそんなことを少しも考えないで、自分本意に注文してしまう男もいましたけれども。

　以前、日本の女は、「好きだ」というような言葉、これは滅多に使ってはいけないとされていたものであります。明治時代に、長谷川二葉亭という作家がおりました。この人はロシア語のできる人で、ロシアの作品を次々と日本語に翻訳いたしました。ある作品を訳していた時に、年ごろの若い男女の恋愛のクライマックスの場面がありました。男が、「I love you」という。女もそれに答えて、「I love you」といって接吻を交す、そういう場面であります。

　ここで二葉亭は、女のいう「I love you」という言葉、これをどのように日本語に訳すべきかと考えて、2日2晩苦悶したと伝えております。男の方の「I love you」は、「僕は君が好きだ」といってもいいし、「私はあなたを思っておりました」といってもいいのです。何でもいいのです。

　ところが、女の人の方に対しては、そういう言

Such feelings and ways of thought are still in evidence to a certain extent in Japan today. For instance, a man and a woman go into a coffee shop or a restaurant together. The man says, "What would you like?" The woman answers, "Anything is fine." In such a case, it is the man's responsibility to decide what the woman would like to eat or drink and to order it for her. This is considered the ideal way for a man to act. Of course, there are men who do not give a single thought to what the woman might want and just simply order something for her that they like themselves.

In the past it was considered improper for a Japanese woman to utter the words, "I love you." During the Meiji period (1868–1912), there was an author named Futabatei Hasegawa. He had a good knowledge of the Russian language and translated many Russian novels into Japanese. In one of these novels, the climax of the piece was a scene depicting the love of a young man and woman. The man says, "I love you." The woman answers, "I love you," and they kiss.

The story is told that Futabatei agonized for two full days and nights over how best to translate the woman's answer of "I love you." If the speaker in this case were a man, he could use any number of expressions, such as "I like you very much" or "I have always been thinking about you."

But in those days, there was no equivalent expression

葉がなかった。「私もお慕いしておりました」と、今でしたら、いっていいはずでありますけれども、もし当時、そのようなことをいったとしたならば、その女の人は、教養のない女だということになってしまいます。そして、その女の主人公のイメージがこわれてしまう。

そこで二葉亭は、この女の「I love you」というところをどのように訳したかということになりますが、2日2晩考えた末、到達した訳は、「死んでもいいわ」という言葉だったそうであります。

もっとも、これはずいぶん前（明治）の話でありまして、今の（昭和の）日本の女は、そんな窮屈な習慣はもっておりません。

最後に、日本人の言葉は、よく非論理的だといわれます。本屋の店に入ってお客が、「スペイン語の会話の本はありませんか」といったとします。その場合、（その本が）ないとします。そうしますと、店員は、「ございませんでした」と答えます。ないのは現在の話でありますが、過去の言い方で答えます。これはなぜでしょうか。

これは、答える人としては、「私どもとしては、当然スペイン語の会話の本を用意しておくべきでありました。それを私どもの不注意で用意しておりませんでした」こういっている気持なのであります。つまり、長くしゃべるべき言葉を短くはしょっていったことから、このようなことが起こっているのであります。日本人は、あまりしゃべら

that was proper for a lady to use. Nowdays, she could possibly say, "I have also been very fond of you," but the use of such an expression in those days would have given the impression that the woman was uncultured, and it would have destroyed the image of this heroine.

So after two days and nights of troubled thought, Futabatei decided to have her say, "I am ready and willing to die now."

This was, of course, way back at the turn of the century during the Meiji period. In today's Japan women are not nearly as restricted by custom.

In conclusion, it is often said that Japanese people speak in a very illogical manner. Let's take the example of a customer going into a bookshop and asking the shopkeeper, "Do you have a Spanish conversation textbook?" If such a book is not in stock, the shopkeeper will answer, "We did not." Thus in spite of the fact that it is the present moment that is being discussed, the answer is given in the past tense.

The reason for this is that what the shopkeeper is really saying is, "We should have the book you asked for, but due to our negligence we did not stock it for you." In other words, this phenomenon arises out of a tendency to abbreviate rather than give a long, drawn-out explanation in such a situation, based upon the Japanese conviction that it is always best to say as little as possible. It is this mindset that

ない方がいいと考えられている。このことから、なるべく短くいった方がいいという考えに進みます。

　そのために、こういった矛盾が起こることが多いのでありまして、これは、おそらく皆さまが日本人の会話をお聞きになって、いろいろお感じになることが多いと思います。

gives rise to the type of short answer that was given to the customer by the shopkeeper.

This trend gives rise to numerous seeming contradictions and frequently makes Japanese dialogue sound illogical to foreign ears.

日本人の宗教意識

Religious Consciousness of the Japanese

遠藤 周作
Shūsaku Endō

日本人については、いろいろな観点から、また、いろいろな角度から考察できると思います。私の場合は、そのいろいろな観点の中から、日本人の宗教意識というものを取り上げてみたいと思います。日本人の宗教意識を特にヨーロッパのキリスト教との比較検討の中で眺めてみて、日本人たちがこのキリスト教をある時期どのように屈折して信仰したかということを考えてみるならば、その屈折の度合いが、日本人の心、日本人の宗教意識を表わしているのではないかと私は考えるわけです。

私自身子供の時、キリスト教の家庭に育ちましたので、物心がつきましてからある疑問にいつもとらわれました。それは、一神論、つまり、神さまが一つしかない、というキリスト教が、山や森

S·P·FRACISCVSXAVERIVSSOCIETATIS·V

It seems to me that the Japanese people can be considered from a number of different angles. I wish to choose the religious consciousness of the Japanese from among those numerous points of view. I would like to examine the religious consciousness of the Japanese by comparing it with European Christianity. By choosing a certain period in Japanese history and examining how European Christianity was modified and adhered to in Japan, I believe that we will find it an expression of the Japanese mentality and religious consciousness.

Since I myself was raised in a Christian home, from the time I became aware of the world about me, I was in constant doubt. I wondered how the Japanese could possibly accept Christianity's monotheism—its belief in only a single

や、またその他の神々を、寛容に信じる、つまり多神的で、汎神的な日本人に、どうして受け入れられるか、という疑問がいつも念頭から去らなかった。そういう問題をいつも頭に置いて、キリスト教の、日本人における受け入れの仕方ということを考えていました。

ご存じのようにキリスト教が日本に入りましたのは、フランシスコ・ザビエルの時代でございます。フランシスコ・ザビエルが日本にやってきましたのは、日本が戦国時代の、今から4世紀前の頃のことでございまして、それから、徳川時代の初期に、日本がキリスト教をまったく禁じてしまうまでの間に、いくつかの段階をへてまいりました。このいくつかの段階を大ざっぱに分けますと三つに分かれます。

第1期、これはフランシスコ・ザビエルからちょうど、織田信長、豊臣秀吉時代にかけての頃だろうと思います。この時期のキリスト教というのは、大雑把にいってしまうと、現世利益という点において、その他の日本にあった宗教よりも日本人に愛されました。日本人の宗教意識の中では現世利益ということが非常に重要な要素を占めておりまして、現在でも病気が治るとかあるいはお金が儲かるとか、現世の幸福が得られるということを神さま、仏さまがしてくださることを願う意味での宗教心というのが日本人の中に非常に強うございます。

god—in the midst of their traditional polytheistic, pantheistic mentality in which gods of mountains and forests and all other sorts of deities are liberally accepted and believed in. And with this question constantly in mind, I have thought a great deal about the way in which the Japanese have received Christianity.

As you know, Christianity was introduced into Japan during the time of Francisco de Xavier. This Francisco de Xavier arrived in Japan about four centuries ago during the Warring States period. Between the time of his arrival and the total prohibition of Christianity by the government in the first part of the Tokugawa period (early seventeenth century), Christianity went through a number of stages of development here. These stages can be divided into three general periods.

The first period begins with the arrival of Francisco de Xavier and extends through the time of Nobunaga Oda and Hideyoshi Toyotomi. Generally speaking, during this time the Japanese loved Christianity more than any other religion because it included the possibility of divine favor in this world. The idea of divine favor in this world is an extremely important element in the religious consciousness of the Japanese, and even today it remains very strong—one can ask God or Buddha to grant money, a cure for illness, or happiness in this world.

本当の宗教というのは、そういう現世利益ということをぬきにして、現世に利益がないというところから始まるのですけれども、日本人の場合には、あくまでも現世利益ということが主体になっております。仏教において、薬師如来のように病気を治してくれる仏さまがあがめられるのもその一つの形態でありますし、現代の新興宗教の中で必ずガンがなおったというようなことを魅力として信徒を引きつけているのも現世利益でありましょう。

　第1期のキリスト教も、病気を治してくれるとか、あるいはそれを歓迎する諸大名に南蛮貿易の利益をもたらしたり、あるいは武器弾薬を供給してくれるものに伴って入ってきた宗教で、これを保護し、信ずれば自分たちも利益を得られるという観点が当時の、これを歓迎した諸大名の中にかなり強くあったことは否めません。そして、この頃のキリスト教とは、上から下へ行く観点でありまして、大名が信ずればこれをまた家臣が信じ、家臣は自分の領地における百姓たちにこれを信仰することを許すという、上から下への封建的な仕組みの中で拡がってゆく形をとっておりました。ですからこれは、キリスト教を信じるというよりは、キリスト教が当時持ってきた現世利益というものが拡がっていったのだろうと思います。

　第2期に入りますと、2代目、第1期の子供たちがこれを信仰するようになって、前よりはかなりキ

True religion is far from such expectations of divine favor in this world, but in the case of the Japanese, this aspect has always been the main element of belief. In Buddhism, one form of this is seen in the worship of Yakushi Nyorai, who cures illnesses; and the present-day new religions use, for example, a guaranteed cure for cancer as a draw for new believers.

Early Christianity in Japan also offered promises for health, profitable trade with the West, and a supply of weapons for the feudal lords who welcomed the new religion. It cannot be denied that the conviction that if they protected and believed in this religion they would also profit was a strong factor in the lords' decision to accept Christianity. And in those days, everything was handed down from above in the feudal social structure. If the lords believed in Christianity, their vassals would also believe, and the farmers underneath those vassals would be allowed to believe as well. Thus Christianity spread in Japan, or, more accurately, the promise of divine favor in this world that Christianity brought along with it was accepted throughout the nation.

When we reach the second period, during which the children of the first-generation Christians were active, the

リスト教についての信仰が強くなってきました。しかしこれも、よく調べてみますと非常に面白いことがあります。

　外国の日本キリスト教史、外国人が書いた日本のキリスト教史などをみますと、キリスト教が個人の自覚をうながしたように書かれておりますが、私は必ずしもこの意見には賛成しておりません。と申しますのは、この頃の信仰には、やはり日本の、大きな農村の構造というものが作用しておりまして、村単位、集落単位で信じたり、あるいは離れたりする傾向がうかがわれるからであります。

　村の人たちがキリスト教を信じるのは、特にそのリーダーが、村長が信じるならば、村人もこれを信じ、村のリーダーがこれから離れるならば、村の人たちもこれから離れてゆくという傾向が見られます。そういうところにも、宗教と日本人の、集落との関係というのが、かなり濃く私にはうかがわれるような感じがいたします。

　ですから、この第2期の後半から、つまり豊臣秀吉のあと徳川家康、徳川秀忠の頃から、そろそろキリスト教に対する弾圧、迫害がはじまりますが、こういうとき、個人の信念によって貫きとおした人はもちろんおります。

　もちろんおりますけれども、おおむねは、リーダーが今まで信じていたキリスト教というものを

very fact of their being second-generation Christians resulted in a far stronger belief in Christianity itself than had been evident among their parents' generation. But close investigation reveals some very interesting aspects during this period.

When the history of Japanese Christianity as written by foreigners is studied, we find the claim that Christianity stressed the awakening of the individual, but I am not entirely in agreement with this opinion. What I mean by this is that the larger structure of Japan's agricultural villages was at work in the belief patterns of that time, and we can see belief or familiarity taking hold in terms of large and small village groups.

If the head or leader of a village believed in Christianity, the rest of the villagers would also believe, and if the village head drifted away from his belief, the rest of the village would follow suit. Here also I feel that we can see the strong relationship of the Japanese to their village group and to their religion.

When we reach the latter part of the second period, we find the beginning of the suppression and persecution of Christianity by Ieyasu and Hidetada Tokugawa, the rulers who succeeded Hideyoshi Toyotomi.

And while there were indeed some individuals who persisted in their individual belief in Christianity, for the most

信じるのをやめるならば、村人たちもこれをやめてしまうという傾向が非常に強く見られまして、一時は非常にさかんだったキリスト教の信仰があっというまにガタガタッとくずれてしまったのは、個人単位ではなく集落単位、村単位であったことを物語っているような気が私にはするわけです。

そして、この際、非常に大きくひびくのは、日本人の宗教には祖先意識、祖先崇拝、祖先礼拝の感情がまじっておりまして、かのフランシスコ・ザビエルが日本へ来た時、一番の難関というのが日本人が、祖先と同じ世界に、死んだあと行けないということ、自分がキリスト教を信じれば、祖先と同じ世界に行けないのではないかということを不安がっているということが布教の障害になっているということを言っていますけれども、この集落意識とキリスト教の関係につきましても同じことがいえるような気がいたします。

第3期というのは、もう迫害が絶頂に達しまして、宣教師たちはこの日本から姿を消し、教会もなくなって、日本人のごく一部の中で、西洋精神できたえられたキリスト教が、ほそぼそと受けつがれた時期であります。そして私はこの時期に一番興味を抱いているわけです。と申しますのは、教会もなく、宣教師もいなくなりますと、キリスト教というものを日本人の歯でかみくだいていかなければならない、そうすると是正するものがありませんので、非常に、日本人の宗教意識の中で

part there was a very strong tendency for people to give up their belief if the head of the village made up his mind to abandon Christianity. Thus, I feel that the great prosperity that Christianity had been enjoying up to this time broke down and disappeared so quickly because belief was promulgated in village units rather than on the individual level.

Another important element that was involved at this time in the religion of the Japanese was their focus on ancestor worship and adoration. Francisco de Xavier explains that when he came to Japan, the greatest barrier to the acceptance and belief in Christianity by the Japanese was their fear that if they became Christians they would not be able to join their ancestors after they died. I think the relationship between group consciousness and Christianity stemmed from the same fear.

The third period covers the time when persecution of Christians was at its zenith. The missionaries disappeared from Japan, the churches were destroyed, and Christianity, with its roots in Western philosophy, maintained only a very tenuous existence among a small segment of the Japanese people. It is in this period that I have the greatest interest. This is because, without churches or missionaries, it became necessary for the Japanese to really get their teeth into Christianity on their own. Since they had no one to correct them, their Christianity was free to change within their reli-

自由に変形されていった。これがどうなっていったのかということに私の関心は集中したわけです。世に申します「かくれキリシタン」といいますのは、永い間、徳川幕府のキリスト教禁止令の中でキリスト教を信じていたごとく伝えられていますが、実はそうではありません。

彼らが信じていたのはキリスト教ではなく、日本的に変形された、彼らの、キリスト教と思っている、民俗的な、土着した宗教だということができます。そこにはいろんなものが混じっておりました。仏教、神道、そういうものが、まるでゴッタ煮のように混然として、加えられていますが、私は一時彼らが、それでは一体、この人たち「かくれキリシタン」というものが、キリスト教信者がふつう拝む神さまを、GODというものを、本当に拝んでいたのだろうか、あるいはキリストのことをいろいろ知って信じていたのだろうかということを考えていました。

ところが学者たちの調査によってもはっきりわかりますように、この人たちは、オナンドシューといいまして、役人たちの目をかくれて、一生懸命手を合わせて拝んでいたいろんなものの中で、一番信仰の対象にしていたのは、実はGODでもなく、キリストでもなく、聖母マリアだった。聖母マリア、われわれがいうような聖母マリアというものよりは、彼らの母親（おっかさん）のイメージの非常に濃いものでした。俗にいうマリア観音というのは、福

gious consciousness. My interest lies in the manner in which it changed under these circumstances. The "Hidden Christian" movement is said to have been based upon an underground Christianity in hiding from the Tokugawa government, but this is not the actual case.

What they believed in was not Christianity but a folk religion based on a mixture of Japanized Christian elements. Aspects of Buddhism, Shintoism, and many other things were all jumbled together. There have even been times when I have seriously wondered whether what these Hidden Christians worshiped was actually the same God as that of other Christians, or whether they had any knowledge of Christianity at all.

As has been made clear by the investigations of scholars in the field, among these people who were called *onandoshu,* who folded their hands and prayed fervently, the main object of belief was neither God nor Christ, but the Virgin Mary. And this Virgin Mary was more like their own human mothers than what we normally think of as the Virgin Mary. What is commonly known as the Maria Kannon was actually the child-rearing Kannon from Fukien Province in China, statues of which were worshiped as Mary. They also drew

建省から来る子育て観音をマリアに見立てて拝んでおりますが、また彼らは、そのマリアの絵を書いてそれに手を合わせておりました。彼らが拝んでいた、その絵のマリアというのは、われわれが宗教画で見る聖母マリアというよりはむしろ野良着を着た日本人の母親（おっかさん）という感じです。ここに私の興味は集中したわけです。

　と申しますのは、キリスト教というのは、GODとかキリストを信仰の対象にする宗教でありまして、もちろん聖母マリアというのはカトリックの場合非常に重みをなしておりますが、第1位ではありません。その第1位でない聖母マリアというものが、いつのまにか「かくれキリシタン」の信仰心の対象になったということは、要するにキリスト教というものが、変形したということであります。

　どういうふうにして変形したかといいますと、キリスト教というのは、母親の宗教というよりは、父親の宗教の非常に色濃い形でヨーロッパでは育ってきておりました。つまり父親といいますとわれわれはこわいものとして考えますが、もっとも今の父親はちょっと違いますでしょうが、ふつう父親というのは子供をきびしく教育し、子供を叱ったりし、罰したりするものでして、母親というのは、子供をなぐさめてくれたり、子供と一緒に苦しんでくれたり、というふうなイメージが日本人の間に強いわけであります。

　そういう、普通の常識的イメージからいいます

pictures of this same Maria Kannon as objects of worship. And the Mary in such pictures looks far more like a Japanese farmwife in her everyday work clothes than the Virgin Mary we know from religious paintings of the West. It is here that my interest has concentrated.

The reason for this is that Christianity holds up God and Christ as the objects of belief, and while Catholics do place considerable importance upon the Virgin Mary, she is not the primary deity. The fact that the Virgin Mary became the major object of belief among the Hidden Christians means that Christianity itself was greatly altered here.

To explain just how it changed, we must first note that Christianity matured in Europe as a religion not of the mother figure, but of the father figure, and this father figure is considered an extremely frightening presence. While the father in today's society has changed quite a lot, the archetypal Japanese father strictly educates, scolds, and punishes his children, while the mother comforts her children and suffers with them. These images are still very strong among the Japanese.

The average common-sense image of true Christianity

と、キリスト教というのは、GODというのは、一面なぐさめる面もありますが、やっぱり、叱ったり、罰したり、裁いたりする、という秩序としての面が非常に濃い宗教であります。この父親のその宗教的なものを「かくれキリシタン」、つまり日本人たちは、いつのまにか抜いてしまって、聖母マリア、いや野良着を着た自分の母親（おっかさん）に手を合わせる宗教、つまり母の宗教というものにすりかえてしまったというところに、非常な面白さを私は見つけることができたのです。

　これは、他の日本人の宗教の場合にもいえることでありまして、たとえば、仏教の場合も、中国や朝鮮をへて日本に入ってきました。それが、日本人の歯でかみくだかれ、平安時代から、室町時代になってくるにしたがって、だんだん母の宗教になってきました。阿弥陀さまを拝む日本人の気持、これは子供が母親に求める気持の投影が非常によく現われています。

　阿弥陀さまというのには、非常に色濃く母のイメージが落ちております。浄土真宗の中の、善人も救われ、いわんや悪人をや、という言葉も解釈の仕方によっては、悪い子ほど可愛いという、日本人の母親心理を端的に表わしているのであって、これはある意味では、母の宗教であるということができましょうし、仏教も日本化すれば、母親の宗教になるといってもさしつかえないだろうと思われます。

is of a God who does indeed give comfort, but who also metes out scolding, punishment, and judgment. I find it extremely interesting that the Japanese Hidden Christians replaced this father-oriented religion with worship of the Virgin Mary, who is actually their own mother in work clothes, converting Christianity into a mother-oriented religion instead.

The same sort of thing can be said of the other Japanese religions. For instance, Buddhism came to Japan after passing through China and Korea. Thoroughly assimilated by the Japanese, by the Heian and Muromachi periods it had also become a mother-oriented religion. The feeling that the Japanese have as they worship the Amida Buddha is a strong reflection of the heart of a child making emotional demands of its mother.

There is a very strong mother-image in the case of the Amida Buddha in the hearts of the Japanese. The precept of the Pure Land Sect (*Jōdo Shinshū*)—not only the good but the bad as well will be saved—can be interpreted as a religious expression of the Japanese maternal attitude that a bad child is the most lovable. Thus, we find that in a sense this is a mother-oriented precept as well, and that as Buddhism became Japanized, it also became a mother-oriented religion.

ヨーロッパにおいて父親の宗教として育ったキリスト教が、遠く日本にまいりまして、そして、宣教師も、教会もなくなり、日本人だけの手に、ひそかに伝えられるようになりますと、その骨子となる部分が、いつの間にかとけてしまいました。そして日本人的な母親の宗教にすりかわっていったということが、日本人の宗教意識の大きな面を表わしているのではないかと私は思います。

　もちろん、母親の宗教というのは、キリスト教の中にもあります。特に新約聖書の中にはそういう傾向はうかがわれますし、また母親の意識というものは、日本人独特のものではありません。東南アジアなどでもうかがわれるわけであります。しかし日本の中では、この母親の意識がことさらに強い、ということは別に私が言わなくても、たとえば言語学者の河合隼雄先生などが常に語っておられることであります。河合隼雄先生が心理療法家として日本人の意識下のものをさぐると必ず母親が出てくるということを常々おっしゃっていらっしゃいます。しかし私は別のルートからキリスト教が、日本人の中で受容されて、それが日本独特のものに変形してしまったということ、それがどういう屈折の仕方をするかということを見ますと、やはり、母親というものにぶつからざるを得なかったわけであります。

Christianity, which matured as a father-oriented religion in Europe, was brought to faraway Japan, and after the missionaries and the churches disappeared, it was secretly passed on by the Japanese themselves, during which process it lost its spiritual substance. And I feel that the fact that it was converted into a Japanese-style mother-oriented religion is a revelation of one of the main aspects of the religious consciousness of the Japanese people.

Of course, there are indeed mother-oriented aspects of Christianity. This tendency is seen particularly in the New Testament, and a mother-oriented consciousness is not peculiar to the Japanese race only. It can be found in Southeast Asian nations as well. However, I am not the only one who has pointed out that the mother-oriented consciousness has remarkable strength among the Japanese, for linguistic scholar Hayao Kawai constantly speaks of this same element in his works. He has stated repeatedly that if you delve into the psychological subconscious of a Japanese person, you will unfailingly find a strong mother consciousness there. And even though I made the attempt to take a different route in my investigations into the process by which Christianity was accepted into Japan and changed into such a purely Japanese thing, I found that in the final analysis, I was unable to escape a direct confrontation with this thing we call Mother.

日本文化とアイヌ文化

Japanese Culture and Ainu Culture

梅原　猛

Takeshi Umehara

私は、日本文化とは何であるかということを、この20年ほど、一生懸命に考えてきましたが、このごろ、日本文化はアイヌの文化と深い関係をもっていて、日本文化の研究には、アイヌ文化の研究が必要ではないかと思うようになりました。

アイヌというのは、今も日本の北の島、北海道に住んでいる2万人ぐらいの少数民族でございますが、今まで、この狩猟民族であるアイヌは、日本民族とはまったく異なった民族であるとされてきたのであります。しかし、最近、自然人類学の分野で血液の研究や多くのデータをコンピュータによって処理する統計的方法が発展したために、自然人類学の研究が長足の進歩をとげた結果、アイヌは、どうも日本の原住民ではないか、しかも、

Bear sending-off
festival

For the past twenty years I have thought very seriously about just what Japanese culture is. And recently I have come to believe that there is a deep relationship between Japanese culture and Ainu culture, and that any research on the former must include study of the latter.

The Ainu are a minority race of about twenty thousand people who live on Japan's northernmost island of Hokkaidō. Up to the present, it has been thought that this small race of hunters had absolutely no relationship to the Japanese race, but thanks to the recent publication of statistics derived from computer analysis, including research on blood types by specialists in the field of physical anthropology, great leaps have been made toward the establishment of a belief that the Ainu may be the original residents of Japan, and that their

この原住民の血は、大多数の日本人の中にも入っているのではないか、と考えられるようになってきております。

これまでの説では、アイヌは、コーカソイド、つまり白色人種であるということであったわけですが、アイヌは、まちがいなく日本民族と同じモンゴロイド、黄色人種である、しかも古いモンゴロイドであるということが、最近の自然人類学の研究によって明らかになってきたわけです。つまり、この古いモンゴロイドが、最初に日本に住んでいて、今から2000年あまり前に、新しいモンゴロイドが日本列島にやって来て、先住の古いモンゴロイドと混血したのが、今の大多数の日本人の祖先ではないかという説が出てきたのであります。

また、言葉をかえて言いますと、長い間、日本は、狩猟の国で、すぐれた文化をもっていたわけですが、今から2300年ほど前に、水田稲作農業をもっている民族が、中国の揚子江（長江）沿岸あたりから、あるいは、朝鮮半島を通って日本列島にやって来て、この民族が、先住民と混血したのが日本人ではないかということが、ほぼ明らかになってきたわけでございます。

そういうことになりますと、これまで日本人というのは、純粋な農耕民族であるように考えられてきましたが、狩猟民族の血も十分にもっているのではないかと、私は思います。たとえて言うと、日本人の好きな食物は、大体、魚、しかも刺身で

blood flows in the veins of the majority of the Japanese people of today.

Past theories placed the Ainu in the Caucasoid or the white race, but recent studies carried out by physical anthropologists have made it clear that the Ainu are unmistakably of the Mongoloid or yellow race, just as the Japanese are. In other words, the new theory that has come out of all this research is that the Ainu were an old Mongoloid race living in Japan, and some two thousand years ago, a new Mongoloid race arrived and intermarried with the Ainu, producing the ancestors of the Japanese of today.

In other words, it has become quite clear that for a long period of time Japan was a nation of hunters with a superior culture of their own, and about 2,300 years ago, a race of rice farmers entered Japan from the area of the Yangtze Kiang in China or from the Korean peninsula, and this race intermarried with the hunters to produce the present Japanese race.

If this is the case, it seems to me that while it has always been maintained that the Japanese are a pure agricultural race, we must also have plenty of hunter's blood in our veins as well. For instance, the Japanese like to eat raw fish and raw vegetables, and I think that this proves that we have

す。そして、また、野菜など生物です。このように刺身や野菜など生物が好きだというのは、私は、やはり日本人の中に狩猟民族の血が十分に入っているのではないかと思うのです。

そして、農耕民ですと、長い間、大体同じことをやってきたということですが、狩猟民ですと、新しい獲物を求めて、あちこち狩りに行くということになる。第2次世界大戦後の日本の発展というものを考えてみても、日本人は、農耕ということだけでは理解できない狩猟の精神をもっている。私は、やはり、日本人には、狩猟民族の血が濃厚に存在しているのではないかというふうに思うのです。

今まで、我々は、アイヌを異民族と考え、アイヌ語を日本語とまったく関係のない言葉と考え、アイヌ文化を日本文化とまったく関係のない文化であると考えてきたのですが、実はアイヌ語も日本語と深い関係をもっている言語であり、同時に、アイヌ文化は、日本文化の基礎をなした文化であると、私は考えざるを得ないのです。

私は、3年ほど前からこのようなことを考えるようになって、アイヌ民族に伝わる長編叙事詩のユーカラをはじめ、昔からのアイヌのいろいろな伝説などを研究しているわけです。私はもともと西洋の哲学を勉強した人間ですが、35歳ごろから、やはり日本人は、日本のことを研究しなくてはならないと思いまして、日本のことを研究し、45〜

plenty of the blood of the hunter in our veins.

Agricultural people live the same sort of life for a very long period of time, while hunters travel here and there in search of game. When considered in light of the development of Japan since World War II, the Japanese cannot be understood in terms of a purely agricultural nation, for they show the spirit of the hunter as well. I cannot help but believe that there is a strong hunter strain in the blood of the Japanese of today.

Up to now we have thought that the Ainu were a separate race, that the Ainu language had absolutely no relationship to the Japanese language, and that Ainu culture was entirely different from Japanese culture. But I cannot help but believe that the Ainu language has a deep relationship to the Japanese language and that Ainu culture forms the foundation from which Japanese culture was born.

I began to think in this way about three years ago, and it has led me to do some research into the long epic poem of the Ainu called the *yukar* and the various legends that have been passed down among the Ainu from ages past. I was originally a student of Western philosophy, but from about the age of thirty-five, I began to believe that as a Japanese I should study Japan. And from the age of forty-five or forty-

46歳から、特に日本の古代のことを研究したわけですが、日本古代の歴史書である『古事記』や、最古の歌集である『万葉集』などをよく読んで、アイヌの叙事詩であるユーカラとくらべてみると、どうもそれらが深い関係をもっている。言葉ばかりか、その内容においても深い関係をもっているというふうに考えざるを得なくなったわけです。

　今までは、アイヌ語は、日本語とはまったく違った言語だといわれていたのですが、よく読んでみると言葉の構造は同じなのです。多くのヨーロッパ語の場合のように主語があって動詞があって目的語があるというのではなくて、主語があり、目的語があり、そして動詞があるというように、日本語と構造が非常によく似ている。そして、さらに音韻が似ている。アイヌ語は、日本語と母音、子音がほぼ同じなのです。

　さらに、また、アイヌ語と日本語とは、まったく同じ言葉や類似の言葉が大変多い。特に、一つの言語から他の言語へ移入することが大変難しいといわれる動詞や助詞の類に、同一語、類似語が非常に多いのです。似ている言葉をあげろといわれたら、私は、たちどころに、100や200は、あげることができますが、アイヌ語と日本語の似ている言葉は、100や200ではなく何千という数になるのではないかと私は思っております。

　また、アイヌ語には、自己反省の言葉が非常に

six, I began to study Japan's ancient history, particularly the ancient chronicle known as the *Kojiki*, and Japan's oldest anthology of poetry called the *Man'yōshū*. And when I compare these with the Ainu epic poem *yukar*, I cannot help but think that there is a deep relationship here, not only in language but in content as well.

Up to this time, as I mentioned earlier, it has been maintained that the Ainu language was an entirely different language from the Japanese language, but when you read both carefully, you find that their syntax is the same. Unlike most of the European languages in which there is a subject followed by a verb and an object, it is very similar to the syntax of the Japanese language, with the subject followed by the object, and the verb at the end of the sentence. And its phonology is also similar. The vowels and the consonants of the Ainu and Japanese languages are almost identical.

Also, a large number of words are either exactly the same or very similar in the two languages. This is particularly true in the case of verbs and auxiliary words which are said to be very difficult to assimilate into one language from another. If asked, I could come up with one or two hundred words on the spur of the moment that resemble each other. And I feel certain that there are as many as several thousand that could be found with a little searching.

There are also many words in the Ainu language that

多い。今まで、アイヌ語は、文化が十分に発達していない人々の言語だなどといわれてきましたが、決してそうではなくて自己反省の言葉が多いということから、大変すばらしい言語だということがわかるのです。

日本語にも自己反省の言葉が多い。ですから、アイヌ語と日本語とは、言葉の性質も大変似ているのです。そしてこういう性質の言葉をもっている文化というものは、どういう文化かということを簡単に言えば、霊魂と礼儀の文化であると思うのです。

霊魂を重んじるアイヌの人々の間では、世界はすべて霊でできている、そして霊の一番強いのがカムイなのです。このカムイというのが自然界のいたる所にいるわけですが、そのカムイというのは、大変力が強い。その力の強いカムイは、有難い（尊い）カミ様であると同時に、大変人間を困らせるカミ様でもあるのです。だから、アイヌは、このカミ様にお酒を献げて喜ばす。それからもう一つ、御幣（細長くけずった木）を献げます。なぜ御幣を献げるかというと、御幣を献げられれば献げられるほど、カミ様の位は上がっていくのです。アイヌは、多神論ですから、カミ様の位がだんだん上がっていけば、そのカミ様は喜ぶということになります。

こうした考え方は、古代日本人の考え方とまっ

express self-reflection. Up to the present, the Ainu language has been considered the language of a people whose culture was never fully developed, but this is definitely not the case, for considered from the point of view of this large number of words for self-reflection, it is an extremely advanced language.

Japanese also has a large number of words to express self-reflection. Thus, the Ainu and Japanese languages have strong similarities in the realm of word character as well. And I believe that a culture that has words of such character can be explained in simple terms as a culture of spirits and propriety.

The Ainu, who place great importance upon spirits, believe that everything in the world is a spirit. And the strongest of all their spirits is one called *kamui*. This *kamui* is found everywhere in the natural world, and it is a very strong spirit. The *kamui* is not only a spirit that brings great blessings but also one that causes people a great deal of trouble. Thus, the Ainu offer this deity rice wine and long, narrow pieces of carved wood to make it happy. The reason for the presentation of these pieces of wood, which are called *gohei*, is because it is believed that the more *gohei* a spirit receives, the more exalted its rank becomes. Since the Ainu beliefs are polytheistic, it naturally follows that the higher the rank a deity achieves, the happier that deity will be.

This way of thinking is exactly the same as that of the

たく同じで、古代日本においても、いたる所にカミ様がいると考えられて、カミ様に、お酒や御幣を献げた。そして、また、たとえば木を切るにしても、まず木のカミ様に祈って、どうかこの木を自分に貸してくださいといって木を切る。こうした敬虔な心は、これはまさに、アイヌの宗教です。

一方、また、アイヌの中には、この霊について面白い考え方がありまして、言葉に霊魂があって、もし嘘をついたら言葉の霊魂に罰せられるという考え方があるのです。この考え方は、やはり、日本人の間に濃厚に残っておりまして、何か約束をするとき外国、特に西洋では、すぐ文書にする。しかし、日本では、めったに文書にしない。個人的な大事な約束は、むしろ大体、口で約束をしている。そして、もしその約束を破ったような奴は、けしからん奴だということになって、除者になってしまう。

日本の社会は、大変合理的にできているというか、いろいろ面倒くさい手続きをしなくても、日本人は、集団で何かまとまったことができるということも、あるいは、アイヌと日本人が共通にもっている言霊（言葉の霊魂）の信仰によるものではないかというふうにも考えられるのです。

それからもう一つ、先ほどの敬虔な心とも関連しているのですが、やはり礼儀を尊ばなくてはならないということが厳しく定められています。たとえて言うと、アイヌには、有名な熊送りの祭り

ancient Japanese, for they believed that there were deities everywhere and they offered them rice wine and carved pieces of wood as well. And whenever they went to cut down a tree, they would always pray to it first to receive its permission for cutting it down. The same reverent attitude toward all things is found in the religion of the Ainu as well.

The Ainu also have an interesting belief concerning words. They maintain that even words have spirits, so that if you tell a lie, you will be punished by the spirits of the words you use. This way of thinking is still strongly evident in the minds of the Japanese today. In foreign countries, particularly in the West, when a promise is made, it is immediately put down in writing. But in Japan, such contracts are very seldom made. Important promises between individuals are almost always made in verbal form only. And anybody who breaks such a promise is ostracized as a disgrace to the community.

It is said that Japanese society is extremely logical, and the reason the Japanese are so good at working efficiently in groups without bothersome formalities may well be their belief in this miraculous power of language, which they hold in common with the Ainu.

There is one more thing I would like to mention in relation to the reverent attitude I spoke of earlier. It is the strict rules of reverence toward propriety. For instance, the Ainu have a famous festival for the sending off of the bear, as they

というのがありますが、熊は実はカミ様なのです。熊は、カミ様が仮面をかぶってやってきたもの。熊送りの祭りは、その仮面をかぶってやってきたカミ様である熊を殺すことによって、その仮面をはいでカミの国に送り届けるという儀式ですから、できるだけ恭しく届けないと、カミの国へ熊は届かないかもしれない。また、送り届けられたとしても、喜んで送ってもらったという意識をもってもらわないと、カミは、また熊の形になって人の世に現われてくれない。それでは猟をすることができないということになりますので、礼儀にかなったやり方でカミ送りをしなくてはなりません。

　カミを送る儀式は、古代日本だけでなく、今日の日本でもありますが、それは、やはり非常に礼儀にかなったものでなくてはならないわけです。

　私は、霊魂と礼儀の二つこそは、日本文化の最も優れたものだと思います。すでに、古く西暦3世紀に中国から日本に使いが参りまして、この中国の使いは、やはり、日本は霊魂の国であると同時に礼儀の国であるというふうに、自分が見た当時の日本を、書物（『魏志倭人伝』）の中で報告しております。

　また、西暦6世紀後半から7世紀前半にかけて日本文化に大きな足跡を残した聖徳太子の思想もやはり、この霊魂と礼儀の思想でして、したがって彼が仏教を崇拝し礼儀を尊ぶということになります。

believe that the bear is a god. To them, the bear-god has come down to earth in a mask. This bear-sending-off festival is a ceremony in which the bear is killed in order to take the mask off the god and send him back to his homeland. Thus, if he is not sent off with reverence, they fear that the bear may not be able to reach his homeland in the sky. They also believe that even though he is able to reach his homeland, if he is not made to feel that he was sent off with joy, the deity may not take the form of a bear again to come to visit the world of human beings. This would mean that the people would not be able to hunt anymore. Thus, they send the deity off with the greatest possible decorum and reverence.

There are ceremonies for the sending-off of deities in Japan today as well, and they must be performed with great respect and decorum.

I believe that spirits and propriety are the two best elements of Japanese culture. As far back as the third century A.D., an envoy was sent to Japan from China, and in the report he made concerning what he saw here he spoke of Japan as a nation of spirits and propriety.

The philosophy of Prince Shōtoku, who exerted such a great influence on Japanese culture during the last half of the sixth and the first half of the seventh centuries, was also one of spirits and propriety. He believed in Buddhism and held great respect for its rituals.

あるいは、みなさんご存知の日本文化のエッセンスとされる茶道と能にしても、茶道は、礼儀の道です。そしてもう一方の能は、霊魂の芸術です。

　そのように考えてきますと、私は、アイヌの文化と、古い日本の文化は、この霊魂と礼儀の文化であって、この文化がアイヌに残っている。また一方、日本文化の中においてもその精神的な骨格をなしていると思うのです。
　私は、今後の日本文化研究は、アイヌ文化の研究なくしては不可能であると思っております。

Even in the two arts that everyone knows as the essence of Japanese culture—the tea ceremony and the Nō drama—we find that the tea ceremony is the way of propriety, while the Nō drama is the art of the spirits.

Considered in this manner, I believe that both the Ainu culture and the ancient culture of Japan were cultures of spirits and propriety, and that this is still very much a part of the life of the Ainu as well as the spiritual framework of present-day Japanese culture.

Thus, I believe that research into Japanese culture cannot progress in the future without delving into Ainu culture as well.

日本文化の二面性

The Duality of
Japanese Culture

平川祐弘
Sukehiro Hirakawa

どこの国でもお札にはその国の偉人や聖人が選ばれるようです。日本でも長い間1万円札と、5000円札には7世紀のはじめ日本に仏教を弘め、すぐれた政治を行なった聖徳太子が印刷されていました。また1000円札には明治維新の元勲で、19世紀後半の日本の近代化のためにつくした政治家の伊藤博文が印刷されていました。

ところが日本では1984年の11月から、1万円札には福沢諭吉が、5000円札には新渡戸稲造が、1000円札には夏目漱石が登場することになりました。私は聖徳太子のような伝説的な聖人ともいうべき

It appears that all the nations of the world choose their great or saintly persons to grace their banknotes. For quite a long time, Japan's ten thousand and five thousand yen notes had borne the portrait of Prince Shōtoku, who worked for the spread of Buddhism, served as imperial regent, and proved himself a superior politician during the sixth and seventh centuries. And the face of Hirobumi Itō, veteran statesman of the Meiji Restoration and noted politician who worked untiringly for the modernization of Japan during the last half of the nineteenth century, had been printed on the one thousand yen notes.

But since November 1984, Yukichi Fukuzawa has appeared on the ten thousand yen note, Inazō Nitobe on the five thousand yen note, and Sōseki Natsume on the one thousand yen note. I personally feel that it is a matter of great

太子や、伊藤博文のような開明的な大政治家が日本のお札から姿を消すことを非常に残念に思うものですが、今回新たに選ばれた福沢諭吉、新渡戸稲造、夏目漱石がいったい何を意味するのか、をここで解き明かしてみたいと思います。そしてその3人によって代表される日本とはいかなる特徴をもつ国であり、文化の国であるかについてもお話ししてみたいと思います。

　日本という国の特色は、日本が一面では西洋起源の近代文明を取り入れた高度に産業の発達した国でありながら、他面では日本固有の文化を維持している国、いいかえると二重文化の国だということです。欧米諸国以外の国で日本ほど産業文明が発達している国はほかにありません。

　それは日本が過去1世紀半来、一面では国家としての独立を保ち、民族としての統一を維持しながら、他面では西洋文化を熱心に学び、よきを取り悪しきを捨てて新しい日本文化を創り出したからでした。

　ところで今回、日本のお札に現われる3人の偉人はいずれも19世紀から20世紀にかけて、日本が

regret that Prince Shōtoku, who could almost be referred to as a saintly imperial prince, and Hirobumi Itō, who was an important liberal politician, have disappeared from Japan's banknotes. So I would like to spend this time today in an attempt to explain the significance of the three men who appear on the new banknotes—Yukichi Fukuzawa, Inazō Nitobe, and Sōseki Natsume. I will also attempt to explain just what sort of nation Japan is and what sort of culture it has based upon the significance of these three men.

The most unique feature of Japan is that while on the one hand it has accepted the modern culture of the West and developed advanced industries based upon what it has learned, it has at the same time maintained its own unique culture. In other words, we can speak of Japan as a nation with a dual culture. Outside of the industrialized nations of Europe and America, there is no other country in the entire world that has achieved such a high level of development in industry.

The reason this has been possible is that while Japan has continued assiduously to learn everything it could from Western civilization for the past century and a half, it has, on the other hand, made equally concerted efforts to maintain its independence as a nation, to protect the unity of its people as a race, and to accept the good and reject the bad as it went about creating a new culture for itself.

The three men who appear on Japan's new banknotes were active during the late nineteenth and early twentieth

圧倒的な西洋文明の衝撃を受けた時、世界の中の日本について思想面や教育面や文学面でいろいろ考え、さまざまな著作をあらわした人たちでした。

　まず福沢諭吉は1835年、下級武士の次男として九州に生まれ、日本人としてはじめて本格的に英語を勉強しました。日本が最初の使節をアメリカへ派遣したのは1860年のことですが、福沢はその船の司令官の従僕として乗りこみ、サンフランシスコへ渡ります。その時、福沢が買ったウェブスターの辞書が、日本へ持ちこまれた最初の英語の辞書だといわれています。福沢はそのようにして英語の力を身につけたので徳川幕府が1862年、使節をヨーロッパへ派遣した時もその通訳として加わりました。

　日本は1639年以来、国を鎖していましたので、西洋文明の正体が必ずしもよくわかりませんでしたが、福沢は自分自身が見聞したこと、西洋の書物を読んで理解したことなどをもとに『西洋事情』という本を1866年に出しました。

　当時の日本人は、日本がちょうど国を開きつつあったということもあって、西洋のことを是非知りたいと思っていましたから『西洋事情』は初編

centuries, the time when the heaviest influx of Western culture entered and was accepted by Japan. They were men who thought seriously about the situation from the standpoint of philosophy, education, and literature, and who wrote many books expressing their thoughts upon the subject.

Yukichi Fukuzawa was born in Kyūshū in 1835, the second son of a lower-ranking military man. He was the first Japanese ever to make a serious study of the English language. When the first ambassadorial mission was sent to America by Japan in 1860, Fukuzawa traveled on the ship that bore that mission as a servant to the leader. In San Francisco he bought a Webster's dictionary of the English language. This is said to have been the first English dictionary ever to have been brought to Japan. The Tokugawa Shogunate recognized Fukuzawa for his ability in English, and appointed him to the position of interpreter for the diplomatic mission they sent to Europe in 1862.

Since Japan had maintained a closed-door policy since 1639, there was very little accurate knowledge of Western civilization. Fukuzawa worked to rectify the situation by publishing a book titled *Conditions in the West* (*Seiyō jijō*) in 1866. In this book he related his own personal observations of Western nations as well as the matters upon which he had gained knowledge through books from the West.

Due to the efforts of the Japanese to open up their country, there was great general interest in information concerning the West. For this reason, the first printing of this book,

第1版だけでも15万部がたちまち売り切れました。福沢は今は慶応大学として知られる学校を開き、そこで英語を教え、英語の書物を通して西洋の近代文明のほとんどあらゆる面を日本の若者たちに教えました。

福沢自身が『福沢全集緒言』に書いた言葉によりますと、福沢の狙いは西洋文明摂取による日本の変革で、「吾々洋学者流の目的は、唯西洋の事実を明らかにして日本国民の変革を促し、一日も早く文明開化の門に入らしめんとする一事のみ」ということでした。

当時の日本人の多くは、どうかして日本は欧米先進国に追いつかなければいけない、という熱情に駆られていました。日本の英学の祖、福沢諭吉は19世紀後半の日本の文明開化運動の主導者であり、明治日本の指導者たちの過半の知的な父だったのです。福沢は1901年に亡くなりました。彼の『福翁自伝』は英訳もコロンビア大学出版部から出ていますが、『フランクリン自伝』にまさるとも劣らぬ興味津々たる読物です。日本の近代化の歴史に興味をおもちの方々に是非おすすめしたいと思います。福沢の慶応大学からは多数の実業家が世に出、福沢自身もその著『学問のすすめ』などは実に340万部が売れて財を成しました。福沢諭

150,000 copies, sold out almost at once. Fukuzawa subsequently opened the school known today as Keiō University, where he taught the youth of Japan all aspects of modern Western civilization through books written in English.

According to a statement made by Fukuzawa himself in the introduction to his complete works, his aim was to revolutionize Japan through the commandeering of Western civilization. In this connection he stated, "The purpose of we scholars of Western learning is simply to make clear the facts concerning the West, to encourage greater flexibility among the people of Japan, and thus to effect an entrance through the gates of civilization and enlightenment for our nation at the earliest possible date."

Most of the Japanese people of that time were driven by an intense desire to catch up with the industrialized Western nations. Thus, Yukichi Fukuzawa was a major leader in the movement toward civilization and enlightenment for Japan during the latter half of the nineteenth century, and he was the intellectual father of the leaders of Meiji-era Japan. He died in 1901. His autobiography was published in English by Columbia University Press, and it compares favorably with Benjamin Franklin's. I strongly recommend Fukuzawa's autobiography to anyone who has an interest in the modernization of Japan. Many of Japan's finest businessmen have gone out into the world as graduates of Fukuzawa's Keiō University. Also, his book titled *An Encouragement of Learning*

吉は1万円札に登場しています。

　夏目漱石は1867年に生まれ1916年に亡くなった人で、日本人のもっとも愛読する国民作家です。彼の文学作品は、ほとんどすべて英訳され、とくにマクレラン訳の『心』や『道草』はその英語文体が秀れているためもあり、評判が高いようです。しかし日本人が愛するのは『坊っちゃん』『吾輩は猫である』『三四郎』などの作品です。

　この夏目漱石は漢文もよくでき、俳句の詩人としても知られていますが、東京大学では英文学を学んだ最初期の学生でした。1900年から1902年にかけて英文学研究のためにロンドンに留学し、帰国後、日本人として初めてイギリス文学を東京大学で講義しました。しかし創作意欲が溢れるように湧いたために、大学講師の地位を捨てて作家活動に打ち込んだのです。

　日本の国民作家の筆頭に位する夏目漱石が、日本国民がもっとも手にする機会の多い1000円札に登場するのは当然でありましょう。

　ところで、日本と西洋の関係について皆さま方のご注意を惹きたい点が一つあります。日本で英学の祖となった福沢諭吉は、英米の文物制度を日本へ紹介する上で非常な功績がありましたが、福

(*Gakumon no susume*) has sold three and a half million copies. It is this Yukichi Fukuzawa who appears on the new ten thousand yen banknote.

Sōseki Natsume was born in 1867 and died in 1916. He was an author greatly admired by the people of Japan. Almost all of his literary works have been translated into English. Particularly the English translations of *Kokoro* and *Michikusa* by Edwin McClellan are well-known and highly valued for their fine English style. But the Japanese people are more fond of such works as *Bottchan, I Am a Cat,* and *Sanshirō.*

Sōseki Natsume was also highly skilled in reading the Chinese classics, and he was a fine *haiku* poet. And he was one of the first students to study English literature at Tōkyō University. He went to London in 1900 and stayed there until 1902 to study English literature, and after his return to Japan became the first Japanese ever to teach English literature at Tōkyō University. Before long, however, his great desire to write led him to give up his post at Tōkyō University and devote himself to writing full-time.

Thus, it seems only natural that Sōseki Natsume, who is Japan's most popular writer, be chosen to grace the new one thousand yen banknote, which is the currency most frequently handled by the people of Japan today.

But there is a specific point concerning the relationship between Japan and the West that I wish to draw your attention to at this time. Yukichi Fukuzawa did a great deal toward introducing the modern systems and capitalist institutions of

沢自身がイギリスやアメリカ人に向けて英語で講演したことはありませんでした。また明治日本の偉大な知識人で、日本の最初の英文学の教授であり、国民作家となった夏目漱石もイギリス人に向けて英語で講演したことはありませんでした。

1868年の明治維新以来の日本は、西洋から知識を学び、情報を摂取することには非常に熱心でしたが、日本人が自分自身について英語で説明することはあまりしませんでした。西洋世界と日本の間の文化の流れは一方通行的なものでした。その傾向は今日も引き続いています。

ところで、皆さまご承知のように、日本は過去20年の間に急速に経済大国になりました。日本の輸出はカメラ・時計・オートバイ・ラジオ・録音機器・テレビ・自動車・鉄鋼と各分野でめざましく、そのために摩擦が生じているのも皆さまご承知の通りです。私自身も1945年に日本の敗北を体験した世代の一人として、その30年後に北アメリカへ行き、その地で日本製の車に乗り、日本製のテレビを見ている自分の姿がなにか夢のように思われたこともあります。それでは今日、外国において日本の存在がなにによって知られているかというと、日本人よりもむしろそうした日本製の物品によってです。

なるほどメイド・イン・ジャパンのラジオやカセット・レコーダーは声を発する機械ですが、そ

England and America to Japan, even to the extent that he is known as the father of English studies in Japan. However, he never gave a single lecture in English in front of Englishmen or Americans. Nor did Sōseki Natsume, who was the first Japanese professor of English literature as well as one of the greatest intellectuals of the Meiji era.

Beginning with the Meiji Restoration in 1868, Japan showed great enthusiasm for Western culture and information. However, there were no Japanese in those days who set about to explain themselves and their own culture in English. The flow of culture between the West and Japan was only one way. This tendency still prevails today.

As you are all aware, during the past twenty years, Japan has grown into one of the world's great economic powers. And you are also aware of Japan's remarkable exports in such far-flung fields as cameras, clocks and watches, motorcycles, radios, recording machines, television sets, cars, and steel, and the international friction this has brought about. I myself am a member of the generation that experienced the defeat of Japan in 1945. Thirty years after that defeat, when I traveled to North America and rode in a Japanese-made car and watched a Japanese-made television set, I felt as though I was moving about in a dream. Today, the reality of Japan is far better known in foreign countries through Japanese-made industrial products than through the people of Japan.

Of course, it is true that the "Made in Japan" radios and cassette tape recorders are machines that have voices, but no

こから、日本とは何かを伝える日本人の声は外国ではいっこうに出てきません。日本という大国の自己表現は人間的な肉声によってではなくもっぱら日本製のものいわぬ商品によって行なわれている、というのが実情です。

　私ども日本人はなにも日本がおしつけがましく大声をあげて自己主張をする必要はないと思っていますが、しかし世界における第2の経済大国ともなりますと、やはりそれ相応に受け答えもし、自己表現もせねばならなくなっていると感じています。そのような状況下では福沢諭吉のような外国文明受容型の知識人だけでなく、日本文明発信型の知識人の必要がにわかに感じられるようになりました。その際、思い出される人物が、今回5000円札に登場した新渡戸稲造です。

　新渡戸は1862年に生まれ、中等高等教育の多くを英語で受けました。彼は人生の3分の1を外国で過ごし、アメリカ人を妻とし、日本の大学や西洋の諸大学で講義し、16巻の著作のうち11巻は日本語で、残りの5巻は英語とドイツ語で著わしています。ジュネーブの国際連盟の事務次長をつとめた、きわめてインターナショナル・マインデッド（国際感覚豊か）な国際公務員であり、秀れた教育者でした。

voices of Japanese people conveying something about Japan are heard coming out of those machines. In other words, the personal expression of this great nation of Japan is not the human voices of its people, but rather the sounds that come from the industrial products produced by Japan. This is the situation as it stands today.

We Japanese tend to feel that it is not necessary for us to force ourselves upon other nations with disruptively loud voices, but I feel that we must do something to express ourselves to the world now that we have achieved the position of second international economic power. Suddenly I find myself thinking that in today's world we need not only experts on the assimilation of foreign culture like Yukichi Fukuzawa, but also some specialists in the promotion of Japanese culture as well. One person that comes to mind in this context is Inazō Nitobe, who appears on the new five thousand yen banknote.

Nitobe was born in 1862. The bulk of his junior high and high-school education was in English. He spent one-third of his life abroad, and married an American woman. He taught at a number of Japanese and Western universities, and out of the sixteen books he wrote, only eleven were written in Japanese, while the remaining five were written in English and German. He was an extremely internationally-minded official, who served as Vice-Secretary-General of the League of Nations in Geneva. And he was also a superior educator.

この新渡戸の著書は、率直にいって、代表作である『武士道』をはじめ、必ずしも学術的にすぐれた不朽の名作ではありません。『武士道』は英語で書かれたということもあって日本国内で今日、夏目漱石の小説や『福翁自伝』ほど広く読まれているわけではありません。

　それにもかかわらず、福沢諭吉や夏目漱石と並んでこの新渡戸稲造が、近代知識人の代表として、日本銀行券を飾る第3番目の人として選ばれたその選択自体に、今日の日本人の国民心理の一端が示されているように思われます。

　それは、今日の日本国民が、かつての新渡戸のような、国際社会にも通用するような立派な日本人がもっと出て欲しい、と願っている証左なのです。今日の日本は国際社会の動向を無視しては存在し得ません。それだけに日本の代表的人物は、一本の足は東洋におろしているが、もう一本の足は西洋におろしている人が求められているのです。

　その際、外国文化を日本へ伝える受容型の知識人ももちろん大事ですが、日本とはなにかということを外国語で外国人に向けて上手に説明できる日本人もまた欲しい。――そのような国民的願望のあらわれが、新渡戸を5000円札上に呼び出した理由かと思います。

Frankly, the books he wrote, including his well-known *Bushidō*, are not, academically speaking, immortal masterpieces. Since Nitobe's *Bushidō* was written in English, it is not as widely read in Japan today as the novels of Sōseki Natsume and the autobiography of Yukichi Fukuzawa.

And I am convinced that in spite of this fact, the choice of Nitobe alongside Yukichi Fukuzawa and Sōseki Natsume as one of the three typical intellectuals of modern Japan to grace the Bank of Japan's currency tells us a great deal about the psychological makeup of the minds of the people of modern Japan.

I believe that this choice is proof that the people of Japan today would like very much to see more Japanese citizens like Nitobe, who are able to handle themselves with grace and distinction on the international stage. Japan cannot exist in ignorance of the activities of international society. It is for this reason that Japanese who have one foot in the Orient and one foot in the Occident are necessary as representatives of present-day Japan.

Among such people, it goes without saying that intellectuals who continue to bring foreign culture to Japan are necessary, but we are also in desperate need of Japanese intellectuals who are capable of and willing to explain Japan to foreigners in their own language with skill and accuracy. Thus, as I mentioned earlier, I believe that it is the desire of the people of Japan for more of the latter type, of which

かつて世界でもっとも大切な海は地中海といわれた時代が西洋史にありました。その後もっとも大切な海は大西洋だといわれた時代がありました。ところが、21世紀、この地球で、政治的にも経済的にも、もっとも重要な海は太平洋となるであろう、と予測されております。

　新渡戸は、東京大学にはいる時、生涯の目標として「われ太平洋の橋とならん」と述べました。そして実際、国際間の相互理解のために生涯尽力し、1933年、カナダで客死しました。その新渡戸稲造が3人の偉人の1人に選ばれたことは、今日の日本人の、国際主義への願望と国際平和への希求をよく示しているかと思われます。

Nitobe was definitely one, that led them to choose Nitobe's as the face to appear on the new five thousand yen banknotes.

There was a period in the past when the Mediterranean Sea was considered the most important body of water in the world. Then there was a later period when the Atlantic Ocean was spoken of as the most important. And today there are predictions that the Pacific Ocean will become the most important on earth in political and economic terms during the twenty-first century.

When Nitobe entered Tōkyō University, he stated that his purpose in life was to "become a bridge across the Pacific Ocean." And he spent his life in constant effort to promote understanding among the nations of the world. He ended his life in 1933 in Canada. I believe that the choice of Nitobe as one of the great men of modern Japan is strongly indicative of a plea for internationalism and a desire for international peace in the hearts of the Japanese people today.

日本人はなぜよく働くのか

Why the Japanese Work So Hard

西堀栄三郎
Eizaburō Nishibori

戦後日本の製品は非常によくなった、故障もないしアフターサービスも行き届いている、というような日本製品に対する賛美のことばが聞かれますが、それは日本人の中に品質に対する潔癖症、すなわち不良があったら恥ずかしい、心苦しいといった良心の呵責（かしゃく）のような気持があって、みんないい品質のものをつくろうと心がけたから、海外からこのような評価が得られるようになったと思います。

これは明治になって日本が欧米から教えられた思想ではなく、日本人が古来からもっていたものの考え方に基づいていると思うのです。製品の品質のみならず、一般的に「恥」と「誇り」の思想が、日本人の行動を大きく左右しているように思われます。人に負けるのは恥ずかしい、いい仕事

One often hears people say that Japan's industrial products have shown great improvement since the end of the war, that they seldom break down, and that servicing is speedy and efficient. I am convinced that the reason behind this reputation is the compulsive perfectionism of the people of Japan. In other words, their conscience suffers when something they have made proves faulty. Thus, it was the desire to provide high-quality products for their customers that has won them such a good reputation abroad.

This is not a concept that came to Japan from the West during the Meiji Restoration starting in 1868. I think it is based upon a way of thinking held by the Japanese themselves since ancient times. It appears that the concepts of shame and pride, not only in the case of product quality but in all other areas of life as well, are important ruling forces in

をしなければ恥ずかしい、という気持が努力をうみ、その結果いいものをつくるようになった。そしていい仕事をしたときの喜びは誇りとなってさらに努力を重ねるというふうに。

「働く」ということについても同じようなことがいえます。他の人が一生懸命働いているのに自分だけ遊んでいるのは「恥ずかしい」または「罪悪だ」といった気持があります。これは「働くことは善、遊ぶことは悪」という考え方に根ざしています。よく外国人から「日本人はどうしてあんなによく働くのか」と聞かれますが、私はこうした考え方が根本にあるかぎり当然のことだと思うのです。

　しかし、それだけでないことも確かです。昔から日本には「苦あれば楽あり」ということばがあるように、いま苦労しておけば将来きっといいことがある、という将来に期待をかける気持があって、今を一生懸命に働くことになるのではないでしょうか。

　また日本人は、非常に「帰属意識」の強い民族だということがいえます。「家」に対する帰属意識や「村」に対する帰属意識の上に、会社に入ってからはさらに「会社」に対する帰属意識が加わります。

　日本では、いったん入った会社にはよほどのこ

the activities of the Japanese people. Feelings of shame at losing to others and failing to do a good job have spurred greater effort, resulting in superior products. The joy of doing a good job contributes to even greater pride in one's work, and this, once again, encourages one to make even greater efforts, and so on in a constantly escalating spiral.

The same thing can be said of the act of work itself. One feels shame if one is enjoying oneself while someone else is working hard. This sense of guilt is the basis of the idea that "work is good, play is bad." Foreigners often ask why the Japanese people work so very hard. But I think the Japanese attitude toward work is only natural given that they are basing their thinking on the concept I have just mentioned.

But it is also true that this single concept is not the whole story. There is an old saying in Japan: "If there is pain, comfort will follow." In other words, there is always hope for the future as long as effort is exerted in the present. And this, I feel, is also one of the reasons for the diligent work attitude of the Japanese.

It can also be said that the Japanese people have an extremely strong sense of belonging. This sense of belonging is particularly strong in relationship to the family and the hometown, and once a person has taken a position in a company, that company also becomes the object of this same attitude—one always has a place to return to.

In Japan, it is traditional for a person to stay at a single

とがない限りそこで働き続けるという習慣が伝統的にあるために、会社に対する帰属意識が非常に強い。それは「わが社」とか「うちの会社」ということばでも表わされますし、仕事を訊かれたときほとんどの日本人が、まず会社の名前を出すことからも窺えるのではないでしょうか。

　自分の会社のために骨身を惜しまず、ひいてはそれが自分のためにも、また会社の方針を通じて国のためにもなると考えて働きます。そして会社も家族的な一体感を非常に重要視して、親睦といって社員旅行をしたり運動会を開いたりして、社員の一体感を養うことに努めます。

　こうした会社の経営は、昔から日本にあった日本的な徒弟制度の延長であるといえるかもしれません。日本の商家では番頭さんや丁稚さんも家族の一員として考えられ、商家の主婦は、彼らの寝食の世話から相談ごとまで引き受けたものでした。そうすることによって、主人と番頭さん、丁稚さんが一体となって働き、それが店の繁栄にもつながったと思います。

　私の家も商家でしたが、昔働いていた者が田舎から上京してくると、1週間も10日も泊めて面倒をみたものでした。「うちの者」という意識が非常に強かったといえましょう。

company for his entire working life. It is for this reason that the sense of belonging to one's company is so very strong. People always speak of the company where they work as "my company" or "our company." And when Japanese people are asked what sort of work they do, it seems to be common practice to begin explaining their job by giving the name of the company to which they belong.

They spare no pains for their company. They work with the idea that such an attitude benefits themselves and that through policies of the company it also benefits the nation as a whole. The company, for its part, places extreme importance on maintaining a sense of family among all its members, and this sense is nurtured through such social activities as company outings and sporting events.

It might be most appropriate to refer to this type of company management as an extension of the traditional Japanese apprentice system. In the traditional mercantile families of Japan, both clerks and apprentices were considered members of the immediate family, and the man and wife at the head of that family handled all matters of room and board, and advised them on personal matters as well. The master, the clerks, and the apprentices all worked together as one unit, and as a result the business prospered.

My family was originally such a merchant family, and when people who used to work for us would come from the old hometown to visit us in Kyōto in later years, we would always put them up and look after them for as much as a

そういう古来からあった日本の制度とか日本人のものの考え方を基盤にした上で、戦後は外国のよいところをすすんでとり入れて、日本的なやり方で会社経営をすすめてきたからこそ、短時間のうちに日本の産業が発展し、日本製品の評価も高まったと思うのです。

　戦後、連合軍が日本を支配しましたが、そのとき私たちは、アメリカから統計的品質管理という科学的方法による経営管理の方法を学びました。私はそれを一生懸命勉強しながら、一方では日本人が本来もっている労働意欲、勤勉さ、帰属意識、仲間意識、恥と誇りの思想などを大事に考え、人の心の問題を基盤にした私流の品質管理を提唱して、全国の工場を歩いて指導してまいりました。

　最近、外国の方々から日本人は品質管理の優等生だといわれますが、それは日本人の中にそれにふさわしい思想的背景がもともとあった上に、外国のよいところをとり入れたためだと思います。

　ここでひとつ、日本人が教えられなくてももっていた仕事に対する愛着と、品質管理の例をご紹

week or ten days at a time. We had a very strong sense of their being family members.

I think it is the Japanese corporate management style, based upon these traditional systems and concepts, plus the active introduction of elements from foreign countries after World War II, that has brought about the speedy development of Japanese industry and the high reputation of Japanese products in the short time that has passed since the end of the war.

The Allied Forces controlled Japan after the war, and it was during this time that we learned the scientific management system of statistical quality control from America. I studied the principles of this system diligently, after which I went to visit factories throughout the nation to lead them toward the introduction of my own style of quality control which was based upon the American system. At the same time I placed great importance upon the traditional Japanese attitudes of desire to work, diligence, a sense of belonging and comradeship, and the concepts of shame and pride, all of this solidly based upon the issues of human feeling and sensitivities.

Recently, foreigners have spoken of the Japanese as honor-roll students of quality control. And I firmly believe that this is the result of the conducive environment that already existed in Japan, combined with the introduction of effective techniques from foreign countries.

Here I would like to pause and give an example of the love of work and quality control that the Japanese have pos-

介したいと思います。

　先ほどもお話しいたしましたが、私の家は、京都で縮緬問屋をしておりました。京都北部の丹後地方の娘さんたちに機を貸し与えて縮緬を織ってもらい、それを売りさばくという商売です。
　今から60年近く前に丹後地方に大地震があって、当時大学生だった私は、父のいいつけでリュックサックにお金を詰めて、地震で被害にあった村を慰問に行きました。娘さんたちは余震をおそれて小屋に避難していましたが、ほとんど着のみ着のままの状態だというのに、自分の織った織りかけの縮緬と機は、大事に小屋に避難させているのです。

　その光景を見たとき私は本当に感動いたしました。まだ自分のものになっていない機を大事に避難させた気持、また自分がつくったものをいとおしむ気持、自分の仕事に対する愛着が痛いほどに感じられました。
　別の町に行ったらその町は、ほとんど町全体が焼けてしまっていました。家もないようなところで今までどおり仕事をすることもできないので、私は兄に頼みこんで、100人ほどの娘さんたちを、兄の経営する近代的な自動織機の織物工場に連れて行きました。兄は欧米で工場経営を学んできていましたから、能率、能率とやかましくいい、自動織機の扱い方も知らないような娘さんたちがき

sessed since ancient times, without being taught by anyone from the outside.

As I mentioned earlier, my family ran a silk crepe wholesale shop in Kyōto. Our business consisted of lending handlooms to young women in the Tango region north of Kyōto and selling the silk crepe that they made on those handlooms.

About sixty years ago, the Tango region suffered a terrible earthquake. I was a university student at the time, and my father sent me out with a backpack full of cash to visit the villages that had suffered damage from the earthquake. The young girls had all taken refuge in shelter huts for fear of aftershocks, and while they had nothing of their own but the clothes on their backs, they had made sure that they brought along the handlooms and the silk crepe they were weaving.

I was deeply moved when I saw what they had done. The fact that they had saved the handlooms that were not even their own property, and their pride in the silk crepe they had made with their own hands was a clear demonstration of their love for their work.

In another village I found that all the buildings had burned to the ground. With no houses or work buildings, there was no way for the people there to continue doing the work they had been involved in before the earthquake, so I took one hundred girls from that village to my brother's modern automatic loom textile factory and asked him to give them work there. My brother had learned factory management in the West, and he was very big on efficiency, so he

たら能率がぐんとおちて莫大な損失になるといって嫌がりました。しかし非常事態なので仕方なく工場を折半（せっぱん）して、前からいた娘さんたち、新しく来た娘さんたちと分けて織らせることにしました。

　ところが、1週間たったら、娘さんたちは前からいる人たちと同じように織れるようになったのです。生産量が負けないばかりか、品質も負けません。不良品の数が少ないのです。自動織機の扱い方を覚えるにはまあ半年はかかるだろうと思っていた兄はびっくりしました。さっそく原因追究のプロジェクトチームをつくって原因の調査を始めたのです。

　原因はすぐにわかりました。新しく来た娘さんたちには、「一体感」があったのです。同じ境遇の者どうしという一体感がありました。どうにかして前からいる人たちに負けないように、いいものをたくさん織りたいという気持を全員がもっていて、休み時間にも、自動織機を扱ったことのある人を先生にして勉強をしていたのです。また糸がこなくなれば糸を撚（よ）る人に早く早くと催促するし、機械が故障すれば早く早くと修理の人を呼んできて直してもらうというふうにして、一時も機械を遊ばせないようにして生産性をあげていました。

was reluctant to hire girls that had no experience in the use of automatic looms because he was afraid that they would lower his factory's efficiency and cause him huge losses. But due to the emergency situation, he reluctantly agreed to divide the work of the factory into two shifts and split up the work between the girls I had brought from the destroyed village.

Before a week had passed, the new girls had become as proficient on the automatic looms as the girls who had already been working on them. They not only produced the same volume of material, but their product quality was of an equal level. There were very few flawed pieces. My brother, who had assumed that it would take about half a year for the new girls to learn how to use the automatic looms, was very surprised. He immediately formed a project team to discover the cause of this phenomenon and put them to work to investigate the case.

They quickly discovered the cause. It was the family feeling that prevailed among the new girls, the solidarity of people who find themselves in the same circumstances with each other. As a group they were determined to keep up with the girls who had already been working at the factory. For this reason they all had the strong desire to produce high-quality fabric, and in order to accomplish this, they spent their free time taking lessons on the use of the automatic looms from the experienced girls. Also, when their looms ran out of thread, they would encourage the spinners to provide them with more thread quickly, and when their looms broke

前からいる人はどうかというと、責任分担がはっきりしているために、糸を撚る人は撚るだけ、織る人は織るだけ、検査の人は検査だけというふうに、自分の仕事以外のことにはまったく関心がありません。

　ここで差が出てくるわけです。新しく来た娘さんたちは誰に教えられたわけでもないのに、彼女らなりのやり方で自主的に品質管理をやっていたのです。

　この経験だけではなく、その後私は他の場所でも、日本人の仕事に対する愛着や自分流の品質管理を見てきました。こうした経験から、私は日本人に合った品質管理を考えるようになって、電気製品を組み立てる工場では、試みとしてベルトコンベア・システムの分業をやめてみました。一貫して作業を任せることにより、ものをつくる喜びをみんながもてるようにしたわけです。そして、どんな仕事の結果を会社がのぞんでいるかを作業員に徹底させて、その品質のものがつくれさえすればその間のやり方はどのようにしてもいいという自由度を考えました。それには作業員を信頼して任せた。そうすることによって作業員は、その信頼に充分に応えてくれ自主性が育ちました。

down, they would ask the repairmen to fix them as quickly as possible. Thus, they raised productivity by not allowing their machines to rest for even the shortest length of time.

On the other hand, the old group of girls were so highly specialized, with those responsible for spinning, weaving, and inspecting the machinery clearly set, that they had no interest at all in anything that did not directly concern themselves.

This is what caused the difference in the two groups of girls. The new group had not been instructed in quality control, but had developed their own system of quality control naturally, through their sense of solidarity and pride in their work.

This was not the only place I saw the Japanese love for work and their resultant independent quality control methods. As a result, I gradually devised a quality control system particularly appropriate to Japanese people, and tested it out in an electric appliance assembly plant. I began by abandoning the specialized conveyor belt system, and having each worker complete the entire production process by himself, allowing him to experience the joy of creation. Then I gave the workers a thorough explanation of the type of results desired by the company, and told them that they were free to choose whatever system they wished as long as they produced the level of quality the factory demanded. I trusted the workers to choose their own methods. As a result, the workers were able to develop a sense of independence that

任せるということは、最後まで責任をもたせる
ということです。そのために自分のつくったもの
は自分で検査するというシステムにしました。こ
うすることによって「働かされている」という意
識がなくなり、仕事に対する意欲がわいて、次の
仕事の励みにもなると思ったからです。事実そう
した私の試みは、いくつかの会社でよい結果をう
むことになりました。

　このようにして、アメリカ一辺倒だった終戦当
時のやり方も、その後だんだんと戦前からあった
日本のよい気風が見直されて、日本独特の管理を
とり入れる会社が多くなってきました。

　それが成功した大きな原因のひとつは、日本の
企業が日本人の気風に合った制度をとっていたか
らです。そうした制度のもとでは社員の帰属意識
が非常に強いために、あるひとつの目的を与える
と、みんなで力を合わせて頑張ろうという意識を
皆がもつようになります。

　私が南極で10人の隊員と共に越冬したときも、
「越冬を必ず成功させよう」という共同の目的を
設定したら、10人のそれぞれちがう性質をもつ隊
員が、お互いに足らざるところを補いあって異質
の協力をしました。自分の仕事は他の人から感謝

fully lived up to that trust.

Leaving everything up to the workers meant that they had to take full responsibility for the final product. For this reason, they chose the system of carrying out final inspections on the products they themselves had assembled. I was convinced that this would get rid of the feeling that they were being forced to work, which would result in a greater desire to work and make them look forward to the next job that needed to be done. I put this system into practice in a number of different companies with positive results.

In this manner, many factories re-examined the totally American way of doing things that had been introduced immediately after the war as well as the good elements of the older Japanese way of doing things, and thus succeeded in putting into effect a unique Japanese style of quality control.

One of the biggest reasons that this new system met with such great success is the system of lifetime employment which fits the sensitivity of the Japanese perfectly. In the context of the lifetime employment system, the sense of belonging among the employees is very strong. Thus, when they are given a clear target to work toward, they are able to combine their efforts to achieve that purpose.

When I spent the winter in the Antarctic with a team of ten people, we approached the work with shared determination to make our project a success. And it was this singleness of purpose that brought the different personalities of the group together in a cooperative effort. We were able to suc-

されているんだという気持が励みとなって、みんなで協力して初めての越冬を成功させることができました。この「みんなでやる」ということが日本人の大きな特徴であり、日本人がよく働くという原因でもあろうかと思います。

　そして、このような団結は、逆境になればなるほど強くなります。会社の業績が振わなければ、何とかして力を合わせて会社をたて直そうと努力します。経済恐慌が起これば、何とかして不況から脱出しようとします。日本は昔から天災の多い国でした。

　歴史をたどればいく度となく台風、地震、津波、火山の爆発と天災に苦しめられてきています。そうしたときの、力を合わせて復興しようという村の中での強い結びつきが、団結力を養っていったのではないでしょうか。

「災い転じて福となす」ということばが示すように、災いをむしろよい方向に結びつけようとする楽観的なところも日本人の中にはあります。戦後の復興のときもそうでした。未来に夢をもってみんなが力を合わせて協力してよく働いたからこそ、異常なほどのスピードで復興を成しとげたのでしょう。最近の例ではオイルショックがあげられます。日本は驚くほど早くオイルショックから立ち直りました。

ceed in our first wintering project by giving every person in the group encouragement, making them feel that everybody else appreciated their efforts. This sort of cooperation is an important feature of the Japanese personality, and I feel that it is one of the reasons that the Japanese people always work so very hard.

When adverse conditions arise, this type of unity within the group gets stronger and stronger. When business results are poor, everyone combines their strength and works together to rebuild their company. When there is an economic panic, they do whatever they can to extricate themselves from the recession. Japan has always been plagued by natural disasters.

History shows that the nation has been visited many times by typhoons, earthquakes, tidal waves, and volcanic eruptions. It was the cooperative effort to rebuild the villages that nurtured the strong links and solidarity among the people of Japan.

As is seen in the saying, "turning a disaster into good fortune," the Japanese people have a general attitude of optimism toward working to turn the tide of fortune and turn a disaster around in a positive direction. This was clearly seen at work during the postwar reconstruction of the nation. It is because everyone combined their strength and cooperated that it was possible to bring about such an extremely speedy recovery. A good recent example is the oil crisis. Japan succeeded in making a remarkably quick comeback from what

貿易不均衡、経済摩擦などが叫ばれている現在、これから先どういうことが起こるのか予見もできませんが、おそらく日本人はこれまでと同じようによく働き、日本人なりのよい解決方法を見い出していくだろうと、私は信じています。それには経営者がまっさきに「皆で客によろこばれるよい会社にしよう」という強いリーダーシップを発揮することです。

they called the "oil shock."

Today when a great deal of noise is being made about trade imbalances and economic friction, there is no way to predict just what the future will bring. I am certain that the Japanese will continue to work as hard as always, and that in the end they will discover for themselves a positive solution to their problems. I believe it will be industrial management that steps forward to take a strong position of leadership in the creation of companies that please employees and customers alike.

米づくりに根ざした
日本の文化

The Rice Cultivation-Oriented
Culture of Japan

鯖田 豊之
Toyoyuki Sabata

　　日本文化について、これまで、日本人および外国人をふくめて、たくさんのひとが論じてきました。本日は、すこし角度を変えまして、日本人の米を中心とする食生活を通じて、日本文化の底辺にあるものをさぐってみたいと思います。と申しますのは、日本人の食生活の洋風化がすすみ、米があまるようになりました現在でも、日本人の心理や行動はいまなお日本特有の米づくり、米作の伝統に規制されていると考えられるからであります。

　日本人と米といいますと、切っても切れない関係があるようにみえますが、ほんとうはそうではありません。米は熱帯性の作物であります。寒い冬のある日本では、1年を通じていつも米を栽培することはできません。日本では、暑い夏をはさ

A great number of people, both Japanese and foreigners, have theorized upon the culture of Japan. Today I would like to approach the subject from the slightly different angle of the eating habits of the Japanese people, centered around rice. Through this approach I will make an attempt to uncover the roots of Japanese culture. My reason for this is that even today, when the Westernization of Japanese eating habits has resulted in a rice surplus, I believe that the psychology and behavior of the Japanese continue to be firmly based upon the unique Japanese traditions of rice cultivation.

The Japanese people appear to have an inseparable relationship with rice, but this is not necessarily the case. Rice is a tropical agricultural product. Due to Japan's cold winters, rice cannot be grown year-round here. As a general rule, rice can only be harvested in Japan once a year in the autumn,

んで、原則として1年に1回、秋にしか米を収穫することができません。米を日本の主要作物にするために、日本人の祖先はたいへんな努力をしなければなりませんでした。

　それに日本の米づくりは水田でおこなわれてきました。水田にしますと、自然の灌漑用水のなかに栄養分がありますから、肥料をやらなくても連作、続けて作ることができたからであります。毎年同じ水田で米を栽培するのが日本の米づくりの特徴であります。

　しかも、毎年同じ水田で連作するのは、日本の米づくりには至上命令でもありました。1年でも米づくりをやめますと、折角の水田は雑草にくいあらされて、地力つまり土地の力をすっかりなくしてしまいます。日本の米づくりでは連作が可能であったばかりでなく、連作をしなければなりませんでした。日本で米が数多くの食品のひとつでなく、ほかの食品を副食に格づけしてしまう主食の座にのしあがったのは、米を連作してきたためであります。毎年畑に植える作物を変えていかなければならないヨーロッパやアメリカの輪作農業とは対照的であります。

　日本は平野がすくなく、低い丘や山のふもとをも米作に利用しなければなりませんでした。畑は斜面のままでも作物を栽培できます。水田はそうはいきません。かならず水平にしたうえで、灌漑

utilizing the hot summer for its growth. Thus, in order to make rice Japan's major agricultural product, our ancestors were forced to work extremely hard.

The reason they were able to accomplish this feat is that they cultivated rice in paddies in which the natural irrigation water provided sufficient nutrition, making it unnecessary to add fertilizers, and making it possible to plant and raise rice repeatedly in the same fields. Thus, one of the unique features of Japan's rice cultivation is that rice is cultivated every year in the same paddies.

Also, it was absolutely necessary that rice be planted every year in the paddies, for if they were left unattended for even a single year, they would be covered with weeds and the soil would lose its fertility. Thus, we see that not only was it possible to cultivate Japan's rice paddies every year, it was an absolute necessity. And the fact that rice was not just one of many foods in Japan, but its major staple food, was due to this yearly production of rice in the same fields. This stands in sharp contrast to the rotational agricultural methods of America and Europe, where crops must be rotated every year.

Since there is a scarcity of flatlands in Japan, low hills and the foothills of mountains had to be used for rice cultivation. Other crops can be raised on sloping fields, but not rice. It is absolutely necessary for paddies to be flat and to be situated

用水が流れてくるようにする必要があります。新しい水田の開発——新田開発はたいへんな仕事でした。たいへんな仕事に成功さえすれば、あとは毎年同じ水田で米がつくれます。

こうして、日本では、庶民レベルでも、祖先崇拝の観念が定着しました。自分たちがあまり苦労せずに米作できるのは、ご先祖さまが新田を開発してくれたおかげだとの感謝の気持をもつようになります。同時に、先祖から伝えられた水田を毎年連作し、雑草にくいあらされないようにして、子孫にわたすことも義務づけられてしまいます。祖先崇拝と子孫崇拝がかさなりあい、もっとも子孫崇拝という言葉はないかもしれませんが、ともかく祖先から子孫へのタテの関係が社会的に優先されることになります。

ことは直接米作に従事する農民にかぎりません。封建時代に領主が年貢米を確保できたのも、その領主の先祖が新田開発を奨励したせいであります。今の日本は封建社会ではありませんが、日本人の深層心理には、意識するしないにかかわらず、熱帯性作物の米づくりを日本に根づかせた、先祖に対する感謝の気持がやどっております。祖先と子孫の両方をだいじにする精神構造はいまも

in such a way that irrigation water can flow into them easily. The development of new paddies was extremely difficult work. But if success was achieved in creating a new paddy, rice could be cultivated in it every year thereafter.

It was for this reason that even on the level of the common people, the concept of ancestor worship put down strong roots, for it was thanks to the efforts of their ancestors that they were able to cultivate rice every year without too much effort. Therefore, ancestor worship came from feelings of gratitude toward those who had carved out new paddies in the past. Japanese rice farmers also felt it was their duty to produce rice every year in the paddies they had inherited from their ancestors, to keep them from being overrun by weeds, and to pass them on to their descendants. Thus, ancestor worship and "descendant worship" became juxtaposed against each other. Of course, there may not be such a term as "descendant worship," but one of the major priorities in Japanese society was the vertical relationship, passing the paddies down intact from ancestors to descendants.

This concept was not limited to farmers directly involved in the production of rice. The feudal lords were able to expect their annual rice tribute because their ancestors had encouraged the development of new paddies. Japan is no longer a feudal society today, but in the deep psychology of the Japanese, while it is no longer a conscious attitude, the sense of gratitude toward one's ancestors, with its roots in the cultivation of this tropical grain called rice, is still a strong

日本人全体のものになっております。

　日本がよく外国人から子供天国といわれますの
も、子孫をだいじにする伝統のせいであります。
日本では小さな子供はあまやかされ、のびのびと
育てられます。すくなくとも学齢期、小学校や幼
稚園にあがるまでは、ヨーロッパやアメリカとち
がって、あまりきびしくしつけられません。その
子供が大きくなって成年に達し、やがて年老いた
両親がもはや働けなくなったとき、両親に対する
扶養はたいてい同居の形でおこなわれます。いま
では子供が資金をだして両親を有料老人ホームに
入れる、親子の別居がすこしずつふえてはいます
けれども、まだまだ社会的にそういうことはほめ
られることではありません。日本では同居扶養が
原則で、両親のほうも同居扶養を期待しております。

　日本でも、このごろは核家族がふえてきました。
しかし、日本の核家族では夫婦のヨコの関係より
も、親子のタテの関係が優先されます。一家の長
でもあり、夫でもある人が転勤を命令されたとき、
子供が学齢期まえのときは別としまして、しばし
ば、妻子と別居して単身赴任します。親の転勤と
同時に子供をつぎつぎと転校させるのは、教育上
好ましくないとの理由からです。子供の教育のた

force in the lives of the Japanese today. Thus, we find that the psychological structure that includes respect for both ancestors and descendants is still very much a part of the mentality of all Japanese.

It is this tradition of respect for one's descendants that has often led foreigners to call Japan a children's paradise. Small children are pampered and allowed to grow up in an atmosphere of utmost comfort and care. It is indeed true that during their younger days, up through kindergarten and elementary school, there is very little strict training like that imposed upon children in Europe and America. When children reach adulthood and their parents become too old to work any longer, support of parents normally takes the form of living together. These days the practice of children paying for their parents to live in private nursing homes, meaning that children and parents do not live together, has become quite prevalent, but it has not yet received the full approbation of society at large. In Japan, living together is still the general rule, and parents expect it.

In present-day Japan, however, the number of nuclear families is on the rise. But even in the Japanese nuclear family, the horizontal relationship between husband and wife takes a back seat to the vertical relationship between parent and child. The person who is the head of the family and the husband and father is often forced to leave his wife and children behind when his company transfers him to work in another city, as it is considered extremely undesirable for

めに夫婦が別居することを、日本ではだれも不思議がりません。

　ヨーロッパやアメリカでは、夫婦の別居は離婚の前提であります。日本はちがっております。たとえ夫婦が別居しても、子供、つまり子孫の代表としての子供をなかだちに、夫婦は精神的につながっております。子供の教育のために夫婦が別居しても、離婚にまではつきすすみません。日本でも確かに離婚はふえておりますけれども、これは、別の原因によるものであります。

　話を米作、日本の米づくりにもどします。農業の機械化のすすみました現在では、米作は農業労働のなかでもっとも手間のかからない分野になりましたが、数十年まえまでは、決してそうではありませんでした。
　日本の米作の特徴は播種、つまり、種まきですね。その種まきと収穫のあいだにこまごまとした仕事がはさまっていることであります。だいたい、じかに水田に種をまくのでなく、苗づくりのために苗代に種をまきます。苗を水田に移しかえる田植えが必要になります。夏にさしかかるころには、水田にも雑草がはえてきます。ほうっておきますと、米は雑草に負けてしまいます。充分な収穫を

children to change schools every time the father is transferred. In Japan, no one considers it strange or unusual for a husband and wife to be forced to live separately for the sake of continuity in their children's education.

In Europe and America, the separation of husband and wife presages divorce. But Japan is different. Even if a married couple lives apart from each other, their children stand between them as representatives of their descendants, thus forming a psychological bond between them. Even if it becomes necessary for the couple to live apart from each other for the sake of their children's education, their separation does not lead to divorce. It is true that divorce is increasing in Japan today, but the reasons for this phenomenon lie elsewhere.

Now let us return to our subject of rice cultivation. At present, a changeover to machinery is taking place in agriculture, causing rice cultivation to become a field of agriculture that requires comparatively little labor. But this was certainly not the case up to a few decades ago.

The most unique feature of Japanese rice cultivation is its planting methods, and the various procedures that must be carried out between planting and harvest. Seeds are not planted directly in the paddies. Rather, seedlings are raised from seeds in special plots. Thus, it becomes necessary to replant the seedlings in the rice paddies later on. At the beginning of summer, weeds also begin to grow in the rice paddies. If the paddies are left without care, the rice will be overcome

確保するのには、雑草をひとつひとつ抜いていかなければなりません。種まきと収穫のあいだにさまざまな労働が必要だとの意味で、日本の米作は農業、アグリカルチャーでなく、園芸、ガーデニングだと外国人に指摘されたりもしました。

　こうした園芸的な仕事を家畜に押しつけることはできません。米作を中心とする日本の農業では、何もかもを人間の労働にたよらなければなりませんでした。むかしの日本人は、肉食をしなかったばかりか、ごく一部の例外をのぞきますと、家畜を労働力として利用することもしませんでした。日本人があたらしい科学技術の開発の点でヨーロッパやアメリカよりおくれたのは、家畜をあまり利用しなかったので、「家畜よりも便利な機械を」との発想が生まれなかったせいでもあります。

　日本人が家畜にたよることができず、何もかもを、人間がしなければならなかったとすれば、日本人は勤勉にならざるを得ません。日本人の勤勉さは家畜にたよらない無畜農業の日本の米作が育てたともいえます。日本人が勤勉でなかったとすれば、米作を維持することができず、今日の日本人が地球上に存在することもなかったでしょう。

　しかし、日本人が勤勉になるには条件づくりが必要です。自発的勤勉と強制された奴隷労働は別です。日本人が自発的に勤勉になる条件づくりをしたのは日本の家族でした。

by weeds. In order to obtain a sufficient harvest, weeds must be extracted one at a time. These various requirements between seed planting and harvest have led foreigners to point out that Japanese rice cultivation is more in the realm of gardening than agriculture.

This gardening work cannot be carried out by domestic animals. Thus, Japanese agriculture, which is centered around rice cultivation, has always depended entirely upon human labor. In the past, the Japanese neither ate meat, nor, except for a very few exceptions, used animal labor in any form. The reason that the Japanese lagged behind Europe and America in scientific and technological development was because they did not use domestic animal labor, and therefore it was difficult for them to grasp the idea of using convenient machinery in place of farm animals.

Since the Japanese did not depend upon domestic animals in rice cultivation, everything had to be done by human beings, and it was for this reason that the Japanese people became extremely industrious. At the same time, if the Japanese had not been industrious, they would have been unable to maintain rice cultivation, and the Japanese nation would most likely have disappeared from the face of the earth.

However, certain conditions were necessary for the Japanese to become industrious. Voluntary industriousness and forced slave labor are two very different matters. It was the Japanese family system that provided the conditions for the nurturing of voluntary industriousness among the Japanese.

たとえば、米作に欠かせない雑草とのたたかい
をみてもわかります。雑草は地上の眼にみえる部
分だけをつみとっても、何もなりません。根元か
ら抜かなければなりません。それには気心の知れ
た家族労働がなによりです。見知らぬ他人にたの
めば、どんな手抜きをされるかわかりません。祖
先と子孫をだいじにする日本では、家族労働がも
っとも質のよい労働力と考えられました。

　もっとも、実際問題として、家族労働だけです
べてのやりくりはつきません。農繁期には他人の
助けが必要になります。そんなとき、家族外の他
人を家族なみに待遇する、家族的待遇をするのが
しきたりになりました。家族的待遇をすれば、手
抜きはしないだろうとの了解からです。家族的待
遇とは優遇することで、他人のプライバシーを侵
害する行為とはうけとめられませんでした。

　家族労働をもっとも質のよいものと考え、止む
を得なければ、家族的待遇で処理しようとした日
本人の伝統は、米作以外の分野にも浸透していき
ました。日本人の勤勉さがもっとも能率的に発揮
されるのは、家族的雰囲気、アット・ホームな雰
囲気のもとにおいてです。日本の近代化にあたっ
て、どの職場でも、家族的雰囲気づくりに懸命に
なりました。日本の企業における終身雇用制、年
功序列賃金制はこうして生まれたものです。

This can be understood by looking at the necessary war against weeds in rice cultivation. If you cut off only the part of the weed seen above ground by the naked eye, it will do no good. They must be pulled out by the roots. This is best carried out using family labor. If you hire the labor of strangers, there is no way of knowing the extent of their negligence in performing the work. In Japan, where ancestors and descendants are considered so very important, it is believed that family labor is the highest quality of labor.

But, of course, it is not possible to carry out all the necessary work with family labor alone. During the busy season, the help of strangers becomes necessary. At such times, people who are brought in to help with the labor are treated exactly the same as family members. This tradition comes from the idea that people who are treated like family will not intentionally neglect their work. It was not considered an invasion of the privacy of such persons to go to extremes in treating them like family members.

Since the Japanese were unable to rid themselves of the idea that family labor was the best kind of labor, it became the tradition of the Japanese people to handle all types of business, even in fields other than rice production, in accordance with this same concept of treating all fellow workers like family. Japanese industriousness is seen at its highest level of efficiency within the family atmosphere, where everyone feels the most at home. Thus, in the process of modernization, the earnest attempt to create a family atmosphere

日本の企業が家族に似たようなものだとすれ
ば、新入社員は子供のようなものです。企業内で
働きながらさまざまな訓練をうけます。いろいろ
な職種をつぎつぎに経験させられます。そうした
経過ののちに、優秀な人が経営幹部になります。
日本の企業ではひとつの職種しかこなせないスペ
シャリストよりも、各種の職種を幅広く展望でき
るジェネラリストの方が好まれます。家畜を労働
力として利用する伝統が弱く、何もかもを人間が
しなければならなかった日本人の過去がここにも
投影されているのではないでしょうか。

　さきにも申しましたように、あたらしい科学技
術の開発の点では、日本人は遅れたかもしれませ
ん。ところが、いちど出発した科学技術は皮肉な
ことに半ば自動的に次々と発展していきます。科
学技術の発展に並行してあたらしい職種が誕生
し、むかしからの職種のなかには必要でなくなる
ものがでてきます。新旧職種の交代を避けること
はできません。

　そうした新旧職種の交代は家族主義的な日本の
企業ではスムーズにおこなわれます。不要になっ

郵 便 は が き

1 1 2 - 8 7 9 0

東京都文京区音羽一丁目

十七番十四号

講談社

インターナショナル　行

愛読者カード係

|||ı|ı|ı|ıı|ıııı||ıı|ıı—ı|ı—ı|ı—ı|ı—ı|ı—ı|ı—ı|ı—ı|||ı|||

★この本についてお気づきの点、ご感想などをお教えください。

本のタイトルを
お書きください

愛読者カード

ご愛読ありがとうございました。下の項目についてご意見をお聞かせ
頂きたく、ご記入のうえご投函くださいますようお願いいたします。

a　ご住所　　　　　　　　　　　　　　〒□□□-□□□□

b　お名前　　　　　　　　　　　　　年齢　（　　）歳

　　　　　　　　　　　　　　　　　性別　1 男性　2 女性

c　ご職業　1 生徒・学生（小、中、高、大、その他）　2 会社員
　　　　　3 自営(商工、農林漁、サービス、その他)　4 公務員　5 教職員
　　　　　6 自由業(　　　　　　　　　)　7 無職(主婦、家事手伝い、その他)
　　　　　8 その他(　　　　　　　　)

d　本書をどこでお知りになりましたか。
　　　1 新聞広告(新聞名　　　　　　)　2 雑誌広告(雑誌名　　　　　　)
　　　3 書評(書名　　　　　)　4 実物を見て　5 人にすすめられて
　　　6 その他(　　　　　　　　　　)

e　どんな本を対訳で読みたいか、お教えください。

f　どんな分野の英語学習書を読みたいか、お教えください。

御協力ありがとうございました。

was found in all fields of endeavor. The lifetime employment and longevity pay scale systems of Japanese industry were born from this same concept.

If we are to think of the Japanese company as being similar to a family, we see that new company members are to the company what children are to the family. They receive on-the-job training within the company. They are given experience in all sorts of jobs one after the other. As they undergo this process of training, the more capable employees become operation executives. Within the context of Japanese industry, the generalist who has gained an overview of a large number of different jobs is preferred over the specialist who is good at only a single kind of work. Here we see a reflection of the past traditions of Japan, in which there was little use of farm animal labor, resulting in the necessity for human beings to do all the work.

As I mentioned earlier, it may be correct to say that the Japanese lagged behind the rest of the world in the early phases of scientific and technological development. But once they got started, it is ironic to note that their progress in scientific technology appeared to be almost automatic. Along with scientific and technological development, new occupations were born, and there were many older occupations that became obsolete. Thus, it became impossible to avoid the changeover from old to new types of work.

Within the familialism of Japanese industry, this changeover went very smoothly. The employees who were

た職種の従業員は別に心配することはありません。企業がお金をだして、あたらしい職種につけるように再訓練してくれます。日本の労働組合は企業を超えた職種別組合でなく、いろいろな職種をふくんだ企業単位の組織になっております。企業があたらしい技術を導入するのにあまり反対しません。日本人は科学技術の開発には弱かったかもしれませんが、科学技術の発展には大きな適応能力をもっております。日本企業が優秀な製品をつくるようになったのは、このような事情が背景にあったればこそであります。

これに対して、科学技術の先進国のヨーロッパやアメリカは、逆に停滞しております。重労働はなるべく家畜におしつけ、人間はある特定の職種だけに従事しようとする伝統が、裏目にでております。科学技術が半ば自動的に発展しつつある現在では、不要になった古い職種の整理が労使対立の争点になっております。

ただ、日本はよいことずくめではありません。長所は短所に通じます。家族的雰囲気、アット・ホームな雰囲気のもとで、もっとも能率を発揮する日本人は、一種の集団主義に支配されております。職場ではひたすら協調が重視され、あまり自己主張をいたしません。自己主張の強すぎる人物

involved in obsolete lines of work had nothing to worry about, for their company paid for their training in the necessary techniques to carry out new jobs. Japan's labor unions are not made up of separate work-type unions that cross over between industries, but are rather groups within a single industry that are made up of a number of work-types. The industries do not put up much resistance to the introduction of new technology. It may be true that the Japanese used to be weak in the field of technological development, but they have great abilities in the application of new technologies. It was against these background conditions that Japanese industry was able to begin producing superior products.

In contrast, the technology of industrialized nations in Europe and America has entered a phase of stagnation. This is a phenomenon produced by traditions which leave all heavy labor up to domestic animals, giving human beings only a few specialized jobs to do. In these nations today, where scientific technology is developing almost automatically, the main point of contention between labor and management is the way to deal with old types of work that have, as a result, become obsolete.

But everything in Japan is not on the positive side. There are both good points and bad points. The Japanese who are able to do their most efficient work in the family or at-home atmosphere are, as a result, controlled by a sort of groupism. Harmony in the work environment is strongly stressed, and there is very little self-assertion on the part of the individual.

は敬遠されます。

　したがいまして、国際化社会のなかで、日本人のビジネスマンは大きな矛盾に直面しております。日本国内ではひたすら協調第一主義で、自己主張をおさえなければなりません。海外にでると、そうはいきません。個人主義の強いヨーロッパやアメリカの植民地だった地域では、自己主張をしない人物は、自分の意見をもたない平凡人とみなされます。自己主張と自己主張のぶつかりあいのなかで、お互いの妥協点をさがしていくのが当たり前です。積極的に自己主張することが要求されます。

　ところが、海外生活のあいだに身につけた自己主張は、日本に帰国するとさしひかえなければなりません。海外と同じ行動をとったのでは日本の社会では通用しません。問題は当のビジネスマンにかぎりません。海外で自己主張するように教育されたビジネスマンの子女は、帰国後、日本社会に適応するのにたいへんな苦労をしております。日本社会ないしは日本文化は、重大な転機にたたされているのです。

　いずれにしましても、日本人の米離れの影響を過大に評価はできません。一般に先進国では、日本をもふくめまして穀物の消費が最近急激に減っ

People who have too strong a sense of individuality are considered undesirable.

As a result, in the midst of the internationalizing society, the Japanese businessman is faced with a great contradiction. At home in Japan, it is always "harmony first," and self-assertion must be suppressed. But in foreign countries, this is not the way things go. In Europe and America, where the cult of individualism is strong, people in places colonized by those countries who do not assert themselves are considered common and ordinary, lacking in personal opinions. It is considered natural for people to experience collisions between their own self-assertion and that of others as a method for discovering points upon which they can compromise. In those nations, active self-assertion is an absolute necessity.

But when the Japanese businessman gains a sense of self-assertion during a period of work abroad, he must learn to suppress it when he comes back home to Japan. The sort of behavior that is necessary abroad does not work in Japanese society. This problem lies not only with the Japanese businessman himself, but also with his wife and his children who have been educated abroad. These members of the family also have an extremely difficult time adjusting after they return home to Japan. Thus, Japanese society and Japanese culture stand at an important turning point today.

In any case, the influence of a departure from the rice-centered culture by the people of Japan should not be over-estimated as an important factor in modern life. Generally

ておりますが、日本とヨーロッパやアメリカでは原因がちがいます。ヨーロッパやアメリカでは肉類の消費が増えてパンを食べなくなりました。日本では米がめん類やパンにとってかわられた面が大きく、穀物の消費はヨーロッパやアメリカの2倍はあります。めん類やパンもごはんと同じく主食的に食べております。このことが日本人の国際化にどのように関係するのか、今後の重要な課題といえるのではないでしょうか。

speaking, in all the industrialized nations including Japan the consumption of grains has sharply decreased in recent years, but the reasons for this decrease are different in Japan than in Europe and America. In Europe and America, meat consumption has increased, and people have come to eat less bread. But in Japan, noodles and bread have taken over from rice on a large scale, resulting in Japanese consumption of grains being recorded as double that in Europe and America. Noodles and bread are being consumed as a staple food in the same way as rice. The effect this will have on the internationalization of the Japanese people is an important issue for the future.

狂言の心
The Essence of *Kyōgen*

野村万作
Mansaku Nomura

狂言とは、もともと面白い言葉、冗談という意味の言葉ですが、後に芝居、劇のことを指すようにもなりました。

狂言は、そのふた子の兄弟にも譬えられる能と同じく、中国から渡ってきた散楽という芸能と日本古来の芸能が一つになってできたもののようです。それは、13世紀から14世紀ごろのこと、室町時代だといわれますから、今から600年も前のことになります。

能と狂言は、外側の形式はかなり似ていますが、中身は対照的な演劇です。よくいわれるように、能は、いわばオペラとバレエが一緒になった歌舞劇で、亡霊の登場も多く、宗教的、神秘的な世界

Bōshibari

The word *kyōgen* originally meant humorous words or jests, but later on it came to be used as a generic term for drama and theater in general.

The performing art known today as *kyōgen* was developed as a twin art with the Nō drama through an amalgamation of the imported Chinese *sangaku* and the indigenous traditional performing arts passed down since ancient times in Japan. Nō and *kyōgen* are said to have reached the form in which we know them today during the Muromachi period in the thirteenth and fourteenth centuries—around six hundred years ago.

The outward forms of Nō and *kyōgen* are very similar in appearance, but their contents stand in direct contrast with each other. The Nō is a song and dance drama which might best be described in Western terms as a combination of

を描いています。

　それに対して狂言は、セリフとシグサを中心とした普通の意味での劇で、その多くの作品が喜劇的な内容をもっています。（この二つの対照的な演劇、能と狂言は交互に上演されるのが昔からのしきたりです。）

　狂言には、当時のあらゆる階層の人物が登場します。大名、その家来の太郎冠者、僧侶、山で修行する行者の山伏、百姓、商人、さらには、スリ等の悪者、そして、いかにも健康な生活のにおいを感じさせる強くしっかり者の女性も登場します。これらの人物が室町時代のころの日常のしゃべり言葉を土台にしたセリフとシグサで劇を運ぶわけです。舞台で演じる事柄も日常茶飯によくある出来事です。

　発生期のころは、リアルな内容に即した写実的な演技だったと思いますが、長い歴史をへるうちに、セリフ、シグサともに型というものが生まれ、芸が洗練されてきたわけで、そこに能、歌舞伎と同様に、伝統演劇としての狂言の価値もあるのだと思います。

　狂言は同じ伝統演劇の歌舞伎のように豪華、絢爛ではありません。3間すなわち約5メートル45センチ四方の舞台の空間に、役者の演技だけで、あらゆる場面を現出させ、人間の普遍的な、いろいろな性格を表現するわけです。舞台装置、音響効果もなく、衣装も簡単で化粧もしません。このよ

opera and ballet. It presents a world of religion and mystery.

Conversely, *kyōgen* consists of dialogue and gesture, placing it closer to what is commonly known as drama or theater, and most of its plays are comic in content. (The traditional practice is to present these two contrasting forms of theater together, in alternating order.)

Kyōgen depicts people from all classes of medieval society. Feudal lords, their top servant Tarō-kaja, priests, ascetic warrior priests who train in the mountains, farmers, merchants, as well as pickpockets and shysters appear. And there are also very strong and healthy women. These characters act out daily-life incidents in the spoken language and everyday gestures of the Muromachi period.

It appears that in the early days, both the contents and the acting style of *kyōgen* were extremely realistic, but as time passed, stylized forms were developed for both dialogue delivery and gestures, and refined into an art. It is in these forms that we find the value of not only the traditional theater arts of Nō and kabuki but of *kyōgen* as well.

Kyōgen is not as gorgeous and opulent as kabuki. It is performed in the simple 5.45 by 5.45 meter space of the Nō stage, and all expression of place and incidents of everyday human life is accomplished through the acting of the performers alone. There are no sets or sound effects, the costumes are quite simple, and no makeup is used on the face.

うに簡素な劇なのですが、演者の力で、あらゆる
ものを表現しようとするのですから、役者の力が
あれば、逆に大変豪華な演劇ということもできる
でしょう。

　ところが、狂言は長い間、能の陰にかくれて、
その価値を充分に認められてきませんでした。能
は江戸時代には幕府のおおやけの式楽となりまし
たが、当時の侍は、（三年に片頬という言葉があ
ったほどで）儒教の影響のためでしょうか、とに
かく笑うことを戒められていたようです。このよ
うな武家社会では、笑いの劇が喜ばれるわけがな
かったのです。

　また、日本が近代化してからの明治、大正のこ
ろになっても上流階級の人々、ことに女性は、人
前で歯を見せて笑ってはいけなかったといわれま
す。演劇に限らず文学でも笑いは、時の政治を司
っている人々に無視されるか、あるいは、その諷
刺性の強さによって危険視されてきた、というの
が日本の歴史だったといえるでしょう。

　狂言が正当な価値を見出されるようになったの
は、第2次大戦後からといってもよいと思います。
はじめに歴史学者が、狂言の庶民的基盤からの発
生を説き、ついで文学者が狂言の文学性を評価し、
後に演劇人がその舞台演技の力強さ、的確さに気
がついたのです。

　その底辺には、戦後の民主主義のいぶきといっ
たものがありました。発生期の庶民のエネルギー

Thus, we see that its presentation aspects are extremely simple. Since everything depends upon the strength of the actor's skills alone, if he has achieved a high level of acting ability, *kyōgen* can become a very elegant art indeed.

For quite a number of years, *kyōgen* was overshadowed by the Nō, and its value was not fully recognized. Nō and *kyōgen* became the official theater arts of the shogunate during the Edo period, but due to the influence of Confucianism, under which a *samurai* was said to smile with only one side of his mouth only once in three years, laughter was suppressed throughout society. It is only natural that an art of humor would not be popular during such an age.

Even after the modernization of Japan during the Meiji and Taishō eras, those of the upper classes, particularly the women, were not allowed to show their teeth when they laughed. Thus, it can be said that humor both in the theater and in literature was either ignored or considered dangerously satirical by the government throughout most of Japanese history.

The true value of *kyōgen* did not receive full recognition until after World War II. Historians began the movement toward recognition of *kyōgen* by pointing out its origin in the lives of the common people, then men of letters began to talk about its literary value, and finally theater people came to appreciate the strength of its acting techniques.

The foundation of this new attitude can be found in the advent of democracy in post-war Japan. *Kyōgen* won this new

を伝えているという観点から、新しく注目された
のでしたが、そのきっかけには、当時の私たち若
手の能や狂言の役者が、新劇の台本として書かれ
た、劇作家木下順二さんの『夕鶴』を能と狂言の
様式で劇場で試みるというような運動がありまし
た。1954年のことでした。

　今まで、能や狂言は無縁のものと思っていた現
代劇の人々が、新しい演劇的な試みを通して伝統
演劇としての狂言に注目しだしたわけです。

　ですから、伝統演劇と現代劇との交流が始まっ
たのは、1955年ころからといってよいでしょう。

　私は狂言を少しでも多くの人に知ってもらいた
いと積極的に行動してきた者の一人ですが、さき
ほど話した新しい試みはその後も続け、フランス
の笑劇（ファルス）で、口のきけぬ青年が恋した
娘は耳が聞こえなかったという、アヌイの『唖の
ユミュリュス』という作品を飯沢匡さんに狂言と
して翻案してもらって演じたり、姥捨の伝説をテー
マにした深沢七郎さんの『楢山節考』を能舞台
で演じたりしました。
　戦後に青年期を迎えたわれわれ伝統演劇人の一
種の試行錯誤の姿でもあるのですが、このような
試みによって狂言の演技の幅の広さをある程度示

recognition because it preserved the energy of the common man of medieval times. But it was catapulted forward through the efforts of young Nō and *kyōgen* actors of the post-war period like myself who began participating in the production of plays that were written for Western-style theater. The first play we gave was *Yūzuru* by Junji Kinoshita. We utilized the techniques of Nō and *kyōgen* for the first time in this play in 1954.

The people of the modern theater, who had up to that time thought of Nō and *kyōgen* as being unrelated to their own work, began to recognize the worth and relevance of *kyōgen* through this theatrical experiment.

Thus, it can be said that communication between traditional and modern theater forms began in Japan in 1955, the year following our presentation of *Yūzuru*.

I myself have always been one of those who have taken an active attitude toward introducing *kyōgen* to as many people as possible. I went on to participate in a number of different theatrical experiments after *Yūzuru*. For example, we had playwright Tadasu Iizawa rewrite Jean Anouilh's *Humulus le muet* —a French farce about a boy who is mute falling in love with a girl who is deaf. And we presented the folk play about a grandmother abandoned on a mountain to die titled *The Ballad of Narayama* by Shichirō Fukazawa on the Nō stage.

In this way, we traditional theater actors went through a period of trial and error right after the war when we were all quite young, and as a result we succeeded in demonstrating

したと思っています。

　私はそのころ狂言の演技は喜劇のためだけでは
ないと主張しました。観客が笑うためだけにセリ
フやシグサがあるのではなく、喜劇である前に演
劇として価値があるのだと思います。だから新し
い試みのテーマも、悲劇的な内容のものを選んだ
りもしたのでした。

　日本国内でのこのような運動と時を同じくして
海外公演もはじめられました。1957年にパリの国
際演劇祭に能とともに参加したのが、私のはじめ
ての海外での経験でした。サラ・ベルナール座で
私は『梟山伏』を演じました。

　山で梟にいたずらしたために、そのたたりで病
気になった男の兄が、山伏にお祈りを頼み、病気
を治そうとします。自信満々登場した山伏が祈る
のですが、一向にききめはなく、ホー、ホーと泣
き声を出す病気は、兄にうつり、最後には祈り疲
れて倒れた山伏も、ホー、ホーと泣き出してしま
います。

　これを喜んで観たのは、天井桟敷でみていた若

to a certain extent the breadth of the acting techniques of *kyōgen* to both ourselves and the public at large.

In those days I kept insisting that *kyōgen* acting had a broader application than just comedy, for I felt it had a theatrical and dramatic value that preceded its use in comedy, and that it was not only for the purpose of making people laugh. For this reason, I chose pieces with tragic themes for our experiments.

At the same time that we began these theater experiments at home in Japan, we also began to take *kyōgen* abroad. My first experience of performing *kyōgen* in a foreign country came in 1957, when I participated in the Paris Drama Festival with the Nō drama. I performed *The Owl* (*Fukuro yamabushi*) at the Sarah Bernhardt Theater.

A young man knocks down an owl's nest when he is hunting in the mountains, after which he becomes ill. His older brother asks a warrior priest to come and effect a cure with incantations. The warrior priest begins to chant his prayers with great confidence, but the sick man shows no sign of improvement and begins hooting like an owl. The harder the warrior priest prays, the more the sick man hoots, and soon the older brother also starts hooting. Finally, the warrior priest falls to his knees in exhaustion and the brothers leave hooting together. The warrior priest slowly gets to his feet and finds that he has also become possessed by the owl spirit, and he goes off sadly hooting as well.

It was the young people in the gallery who expressed the

者たちでした。演技中に、観客席からも、ホー、ホーと真似をされるし、日本では滅多にやらないことですがカーテン・コールをした時は、ものすごい拍手と泣き声の真似が舞台へかえってきました。演者として、こんなに喜んでいる観客を日本では見たことがありませんでした。

そのころ、日本での能や狂言をとり巻く有識者といわれる人の多くは、狂言はセリフ劇だから外国では理解されないだろうと考えていましたから、私はこの反響が大変愉快でもあり、大いに励まされたわけです。

これは、やはり筋が単純であること、山伏という権力者への諷刺的な描き方が親近感を与えアピールしたのだと思います。

その後、アメリカをはじめヨーロッパ、インド、中国とずいぶん海外公演を重ねましたし、アメリカでは何度か狂言の演技の指導もいたしました。

外国においても、日本と同じように、能、歌舞伎は文学としてずいぶん早くから紹介されましたが、狂言の紹介の本はほとんどありません。1963年にアメリカで狂言の演技を教えた時も、『Japanese Folk Plays』という、狂言を何曲か翻訳した本があるだけでした。私はその時も多くの大学で公演をしましたが、アメリカ人たちは、狂言がどんなものか知らずに、ただ日本の伝統的な喜劇であることをポスターやチラシで知っている

greatest joy at that performance. They began hooting back at us during the performance. Afterward we came out for a curtain call (something that is never done in the traditional arts in Japan), and the whole audience began applauding and hooting at the top of their lungs. I had never experienced such an audience reaction in Japan in all my years as an actor.

In those days, the Nō- and *kyōgen*-oriented intelligentsia of Japan thought that *kyōgen* would be incomprehensible to foreign audiences due to its dependence upon dialogue for dramatic impact. Thus, I was particularly happy and encouraged by the reaction of our Paris audience.

I think that the reasons for their reaction lay in the simplicity of the plot line, and in the familiar satirical depiction of the warrior priest who was supposed to be a person with authority and power.

Since that time, I have performed quite a number of times in America, Europe, India, and China, and I have taught *kyōgen* acting techniques in America upon several occasions.

Nō and kabuki were introduced to foreign countries quite early as literature, but there were hardly any books on *kyōgen* at all in the early days. When I went to America in 1963 to teach *kyōgen* for the first time, the only book available was a small collection of script translations by Shiho Sakanishi titled *Japanese Folk Plays*. On the same trip, I performed at several universities. Those who came to our performances knew nothing about *kyōgen*. The only information available to them was found on the posters and fliers for our perform-

だけで会場にやってきます。

　言葉が中心となるような狂言は上演しませんが、『梟山伏』や、酒好きの2人の家来が、縛られても、主人の留守に酒を盗み飲みする『棒しばり』などは動きが面白く、たとえば、長い棒を肩にかついで棒術を使っている時に両方の手首を棒とともに縛られてしまった家来が、工夫してやっと酒を飲めた時の「さてもよい酒じゃ」などの表現は、まるで日本語がわかるのではないかと思うほど同感の反応をします。

　これはボディ・ランゲージといいますか、体全体から言葉を発している狂言の表現の豊かさやセリフに音楽的な誇張があるから伝わるわけです。また手首を縛られているために、酒壺から酒は汲めるのだが、口元へ運べないというおかしい動作などは日本人よりその反応が鋭く早いのです。これは合理的な考えとともに、よく舞台の動きを見つめている証拠です。

　昨年の夏もニューヨークのリンカーン・センターの野外の池の上に仮設の能舞台をつくり、薪をたいて狂言を演じました。大勢の見物にまざって子供たちもいましたが、なんとも屈託のない、天真爛漫な笑い声が印象的でした。

　子供といえば、日本の子供は（小学生低学年ぐらいですと、その素直な感受性が感じられること

ances, which simply stated that it was a traditional form of comic theater from Japan.

We did not perform any of the dialogue-centered plays. Rather we took *The Owl* which I spoke of earlier and *Tied To a Stick* (*Bōshibari*). The latter tells about two servants who love to drink *sake*. Their master ties their hands so they cannot steal his *sake* while he is out. When they devise a way to steal a drink for themselves in spite of their restricted condition, and the servant who has his arms tied to a stick across his shoulders says, "Oh, I must say, what delicious *sake* this is!" the audience reacted with sympathetic laughter as though they understood his words perfectly.

The reason for this is the rich body language and the musical exaggeration of sounds that are found in *kyōgen* acting. Foreigners also react much more sensitively to such gestures as when the servant whose arms are tied to the stick finds it possible to fill his cup with *sake* but finds it quite impossible to bring the cup near enough to his lips to get even a single sip. This is due both to their logical way of thinking and to their close attention to the action on the stage.

Last year I performed *kyōgen* on an outdoor stage built over a pond with torches for lighting at Lincoln Center in New York City. There were many children in the huge crowds who came to see us, and the waves of their laughter that rolled across the pond deeply moved us as we performed on the stage.

When I think of children in Japan in recent years, I realize that aside from the lower grade elementary students whose

がありますが）中学生あたりになると、もう古典とか伝統とかに対するある種の固定観念が生まれ、古典の言葉の理解力の低下もあって、このごろは鑑賞力が低下してきています。

テレビ等の低俗な笑いの影響もあるでしょう。単に、面白おかしい動作に笑っても、じっくりとセリフを聞いてそれを理解してはじめて面白さがわかるような狂言への反応が弱まっています。昔の国語は、読み方といわれたくらいで、教室で声を出して読むことに力を入れました。大きな声で、「素読」をしたから古典の言葉も耳から理解できるわけです。

狂言の言葉は、日本語の美しさを伝えてきていますし、狂言の役者のセリフは、明晰で観客の隅々まで通るように、音楽的な抑揚とリズムをもっています。

イギリスならシェイクスピア、フランスならモリエールの芝居が、その国の言葉の美しさの手本のようになっていると聞いています。言葉は古いけれども狂言もそのような存在であってよいと思うのですが、どうでしょうか。
　言葉を媒介にしている演劇は、音楽や美術のよ

sensitivities are still straightforward, they have come to hold a deep prejudice against classical or traditional arts. Also, the increasing lack of ability to comprehend the older language of the classics among junior high and high-school students has brought about a serious deterioration in their ability to appreciate performances of *kyōgen* and other traditional stage arts.

Part of the fault most likely lies with the vulgar humor of television and other contemporary entertainment media. In any case, while they do laugh at obvious amusing behavior, their reaction to dialogue that demands careful listening to understand and appreciate has weakened considerably in recent years. In the past, our national language and its literature was taught to our schoolchildren by having them read out loud in the classroom. In those days, not only their eyes but also their ears were made accustomed to the language of the classics.

The dialogue of *kyōgen*, with its unique musical intonation and rhythm, preserves the beauty of the Japanese language, and its delivery techniques make it possible for everyone in the theater to hear each and every word clearly and distinctly.

I understand that the plays of Shakespeare in England and Molière in France are held up as models of the beauty of the languages of those nations. And I firmly believe that *kyōgen* dialogue serves well as the same sort of model for the national language of Japan.

It may be thought difficult for a theater form that

うな幅広い海外交流はむずかしいかもしれません。しかし、私に狂言を習っていたアメリカ人が、「狂言の舞台は、西洋の演劇と違って、主人と家来がどんなに舞台の上で争い、対立しても、幕が下りてしまえば、多分、お互いにシェーク・ハンド（握手）しているのではないかと想像されるような、平和な、人間どうしが許し合っている世界を感じます」といったことがありますが、そのような心あたたまる世界に狂言の笑いの本質があるように思います。

これは外国人だからこそ指摘しえた名言です。ただゲラゲラと観客を笑わせるのではない、人間味のあふれた、普遍的な笑いの世界をぜひ国の内外に普及し紹介したいと私は思っています。今年も4月にオーストラリアとシンガポールへ行って、狂言を向こうで初めて紹介する予定です。

経済摩擦や輸出入の問題など、最近の日本をとりまく環境はきびしいものがあるようですが、狂言を見れば、外国人の日本人観も少しは変わるのではないでしょうか。狂言を通じての笑いの輸出は、日本の文化的外交として大変有効ではないかと思っています。

depends upon words for its effect to take part in international communications and cultural exchange on as broad a scale as music and the graphic arts. However, one of my foreign students once said that in *kyōgen*, no matter how much masters and servants quarrel on stage, it seems certain that after it is all over, they are shaking hands and making up again backstage. And in this context, *kyōgen* is indeed a world of peace where human beings always forgive each other of their foibles and go on living together in harmony. I am convinced that it is in this warmly human world that the true essence of *kyōgen* humor is found.

This aspect became clear because this student of mine was from a foreign country. I sincerely hope to continue to introduce this very human world of universal laughter which conveys more than simple humor to all people both at home and abroad. This year I have plans to travel to Australia and Singapore to introduce *kyōgen* to those countries for the first time.

Japan is faced today with serious problems of international economic friction and trade balances, but I feel certain that if the people of the rest of the world get a chance to see *kyōgen*, their opinion of the people of Japan will undoubtedly change for the better. The export of laughter through *kyōgen* can without a doubt serve as an extremely effective diplomatic channel for the spread of the culture of Japan.

心の文化
A Culture of the Heart

井上　靖
Yasushi Inoue

　　　　そ れぞれの国の文化は、独自なものをもって
　　　　　いますが、その独自なものはどうして作ら
れるかというと、これは例外なくその国の歴史が
作るものです。歴史を土壌として花開いたものが
その国の文化だと思います。それぞれの国はみな
歴史が違っている、だから文化も違う。日本の文
化に独自なものがあるとすれば、それは日本の歴
史が作ったものです。

　日本の歴史というものはどういうところが他の
国に比べて独自であるかというと、一番はっきり
していることは、地理的にいって日本はアジア大
陸の東に近い島であり、太平洋の西側の島であり、
小さい島の列島から成り立っています。大陸から
切り離されているので他民族の侵略を受けたり、
そして他民族のもっている文化が日本へ入ってき

Envoy ship to
Tang China

All nations have their own unique cultures, and that uniqueness is, without exception, a product of a nation's history. History is, I believe, the foundation on which a nation grows. All countries have different histories. Thus, their cultures are also different from each other. If we are to find anything unique in the culture of Japan, it will be something that Japan's history has brought into being.

Compared to other nations of the world, Japan's clearest unique feature is its geography. It comprises a small group of islands located adjacent to the east coast of the Asian continent in the far western part of the Pacific Ocean. Since it is clearly separated from the continent, however, there are extremely few examples of other races invading Japan and exerting a serious cultural influence. And it goes without

て日本文化に大きい影響を与えるということが非常に少なかったのです。そして日本文化の一番根源になっているのは、これはいうまでもないことですが、7、8世紀の中国大陸から入れた学問、芸術、文化、広い意味で文化ですが、それが元になっています。

それから、この先進国──当時中国は唐と呼ばれていましたが──の非常に高い文化を日本は国全体で夢中になって取り入れました。遣唐船（ときの政府の命令で唐の文化を輸入するため、多くの使節が派遣された）で命がけで大陸に渡り、そこで10年、20年、長いのは50年も勉強したものを持ち帰ってきました。それが日本の学術文化の全部の元になっています。

それから後、約1000年、あるいは1200〜1300年という間、他国との表向きの通行のない時代がおかれています。そして最後の方の1200年は政治的な一つの孤立です。江戸幕府によって、鎖国という政治的な孤立状態におかれたのです。

その間に、先進国の唐から入れた文化を全部日本独自なものに変えてしまいました。文字も中国から入れましたが、漢字の他に、平仮名を作ったり片仮名を作ったりしました。

saying that the most basic source of Japanese culture as we know it today was the learning, the art, and the various other cultural elements that were brought into Japan from the Chinese continent during the seventh and eighth centuries.

The culture of advanced Tang-dynasty China was eagerly accepted and studied by all the people of Japan. Official envoy ships were sent to China and many ambassadors risked their very lives in the work of importing that nation's culture into Japan. Some would spend ten, twenty, or even as many as fifty years studying their chosen field in China for the purpose of bringing the knowledge they gained back to their homeland of Japan. The knowledge they brought back in this manner provided the basis for the development of Japan's traditional artistic and scientific culture.

For the 1,300 years following the introduction of Chinese culture, Japan maintained a policy of no communication with any foreign country. Japan maintained complete independence throughout this time on both the cultural and the political levels. But the truly strict political policy of keeping doors closed to the outside world was most firmly maintained at the end of this period by the Edo shogunate.

During this long period, the culture that had been introduced from Tang China was completely Japanized. Even the characters in which our language is written were originally imported from China, but from those characters, the Japan-

もちろん仏教も入りました。仏教は入りましたけれども、他の国の宗教の入れ方とは違って、国の政治を改変するような入り方では入ってきませんでした。日本人の生活の信条、考え方の上で、あるいは心の問題として仏教が入りました。

　ですから日本には大きい仏教遺跡がありません。アジャンター（インド中央部マハーラーシュトラ州にある6世紀から7世紀にかけての仏教の遺跡）など、同じアジアでも仏教の通過した国は大きい遺跡をもっていますが、日本にはそういったものはなく、日本人の心の中へ入ったのです。そして何もかも他国との通行のない、1200〜1300年の間に独自なものに改変してしまいました。そして、日本の独自の文化が生み出されたのです。

　では、その間にどのような独自なものに変えられていったかと申しますと、これはやはり日本の民族性といったものに非常に大きな関わりがあります。他国との通行がない時代に日本独自の文化が生み出されている、そういう意味でわりあい日本文化の独自性というものはつかみやすいのです。
　文学でいいますと、一番古い日本の歌集として『万葉集』という8世紀頃、国家が編纂した短歌の詩集があります。これは日本文学史の上でも非常

ese developed their own syllabary systems known as *hiragana* and *katakana*.

Buddhism was also brought in from China, but the way in which it was assimilated in Japan was different from the way in which foreign religions are introduced into other countries of the world, for it had no effect upon the government of Japan. Buddhism was introduced into Japan only as a problem to be solved in the realm of thought and of the heart.

For this reason, there are no great Buddhist ruins in Japan like the Ajanta caves of the central Indian state of Maharashtra from the sixth and seventh centuries, and those found in other Asian nations through which Buddhism passed. Rather, Buddhism entered into the hearts of the people of Japan. And during the same 1,300 years during which Japan had no communication with any other nation of the world, Buddhism was converted into a uniquely Japanese religion, giving to Japan the unique traditional culture we know today.

The way in which Japan changed during that long period of time is closely tied up with the national character of its people. Since Japan's culture developed during the time when there was no communication with the outside world, it is easier than one would expect to grasp the way in which the unique character of Japanese culture was formulated.

The oldest Japanese collection of poetry is the *Man'yōshū*. It is made up of *tanka* verses (five-line poems of 5-7-5-7-7 syllables) that were collected and edited under the auspices

に価値の高いものでありますが、この詩集に取り扱われている内容というものは、死や死者を弔う問題、恋愛、旅の紀行、この三つがほとんど『万葉集』の内容を占めています。

　同じ時代に中国からたくさんの文化を取り入れ、皆、日本はそれを元にしました。文字について申し上げると、唐時代は中国の歴史の中でも、一番素晴らしい詩人が輩出した時期で、唐の時代の詩もたくさん日本へ入りました。しかし、これは日本に全く影響を与えませんでした。

　『万葉集』について申しますと、いま申しましたように死者を弔う歌、恋の歌、あるいは旅の歌で、いつでも自分の心を歌っています。同じ時代の中国の詩というものは——それは大変な数ですが——大風俗辞典、あるいは大風俗資料といってもいいくらいで、全部風俗を歌っています。『万葉集』から“奈良の都”を想像することはできません。“奈良の都”ではどのような服装をして人々が町を歩いていたか、どこが賑やかだったか、一切そういうことは『万葉集』から知ることはできません。

　これに比べて唐時代の詩には全部、当時の首都長安の町が歌い出されています。繁華街も、あるいはハイキングの場所も、そしてあるいはどこで人が群がっていたか、そして牡丹見物の名所にはどのように人が集まっていたとか、全部風俗が歌われています。そこが日本と中国とではまるで違

of the government in the eighth century. This is an extremely valuable work in terms of Japan's literary history. However, the subject matter of the verses is of only three types—death and prayers for the dead, love, and travel.

It was during the same period of time that a great amount of culture was introduced from China and became the basis for everything accomplished by the Japanese in subsequent years. In terms of literature, the Tang Dynasty was the time when China's greatest poets lived, and much of their poetry was brought to Japan. But their poetry exerted absolutely no influence on Japan.

As I mentioned earlier, the poets of Japan's *Man'yōshū* always expressed their hearts in terms of prayers for the dead, love songs, and travel songs, while the great majority of the contemporary Chinese poets wrote copiously and exclusively of the manners and customs of daily life, making the poetry of Tang China a veritable encyclopedia of life in China during that period. There is nothing in the *Man'yōshū* that is any aid in imagining what the Japanese capital city of Nara was like. We cannot learn anything about what parts of the city were the most active.

On the other hand, in the poetry of the Tang Dynasty, everything about the Chinese capital city of Chang-an (present Xian) is clearly delineated and explained. We find descriptions of the business district, of hiking courses, of the places people gathered for pleasure, and how and where people would gather to enjoy the peonies. All manners and customs

うところです。

　日本の『万葉集』で、いつでも自分の心だけを歌っているという、その流れというものは、それからずっといろいろな形で鎖国時代の1200〜1300年の間を流れています。これは文字ばかりでなく、絵の中にも流れています。

　文学の場合では、日本に俳句とか、歌とか、短い形の詩がずっと行なわれて、今でも行なわれています。これもやはり自分の心だけを歌っているから短い詩で充分、自分の心を歌いつくせるのです。ですから、俳句や歌の短詩形というものが日本の伝統的な文学の流れとして、今日に伝わっています。

　それと同じことが絵画でもいえます。花鳥風月とか、山水とかいいますけれども、山や川を描き、花や鳥を描く。だがこの場合、山を写実的には取り扱っていません。いつでもその山を見た自分の心というものを画家は描いています。これは、やはり絵画においても文学と同じです。いつでも描く対象は心です。鳥を描いてもいかに自分がその鳥を、どのように見ているかという、その自分の見た鳥を描いています。鳥がそこに本当にいるように、写実的には取り扱っていません。いつでも心の問題です。ですからたくさんの有名な歌人では、12世紀に西行という人も出ているし、俳人で

of the people are found in the poetry of the Tang poets. This is one point upon which Japan and China sharply differ.

The Japanese tendency to speak only about what is in one's heart found in the *Man'yōshū* continued to flourish all the way down through the 1,300 years of isolationism. This is true not only in literature, but also in Japanese painting as well.

In the case of literature, a number of short verse forms such as *haiku* and *tanka* have continued to dominate Japan's poetry in both the past and the present. This is due to the fact that the poets only speak of their own hearts, and short poetic forms are quite sufficient to express the feelings of the heart. It is for this reason that *haiku* and *tanka* have formed the bulk of Japan's traditional literature even down to the present day.

As I mentioned earlier, the same thing can be said of Japanese painting. The subject matter is mainly birds, flowers, and scenery. But when a Japanese artist paints a mountain, he does not express it realistically, but rather draws it as he sees it in his heart. Thus, we see that the Japanese approach to painting is the same as to literature. Here again, the primary subject is the heart. Even when a Japanese artist paints a bird, he concentrates his efforts on the way he sees that bird rather than the way it exists in reality. There is no attempt to paint the bird as though it actually exists on the canvas. It is always handled as a problem of the heart. Among the most famous poets of Japan are the twelfth-cen-

は、17世紀に芭蕉という人も出ています。例外なく、この歌人や俳人たちは自分の心を歌っています。

それから鎖国の長い間、日本文化が独自なものを形成する時代にももちろん例外はあります。それは浮世絵というもので、日本風俗を描いた絵であります。これは、日本の浮世絵として世界で有名ですけれども、それも日本が生み出したものですが、日本文化の独自なものの底を流れている、一本の水脈のようなものとしてこれを捉えることはできません。日本の文化の独自の本流というものは、今申し上げたように心の問題です。それが日本の文化の特別なものを作り上げ、明治へきました。

明治へきて初めて鎖国を解きました。先進国、ヨーロッパの文化を意欲的に取り入れる時代がきました。これはちょうど1200〜1300年前に先進国の唐から学術・文化を全面的に取り入れたあの熱意と同じです。本腰になって先進国の文化を日本へ取り入れ、要するに近代化を行なったのです。近代的な文化を取り入れて——第2次世界大戦が間に入っていますが——その間にずっと日本の近代化というものが行なわれ、今日に至っています。

今日みると、日本の文化というものは、非常に

tury Saigyō and the seventeenth-century Bashō. There are many others, but they all, without exception, write about what is in their own hearts.

During the long years of isolation, the time during which Japan's unique culture took form, there were, of course, exceptions. One of these was the *ukiyo-e* woodblock print which depicted the manners and customs of the Japanese people. The *ukiyo-e* of Japan has now become famous throughout the world, and it is indeed an art born of Japan, but this genre of art cannot be considered a part of the deep flow that has been the mainstream of Japan's unique culture, for as I have mentioned several times earlier, the mainstream of that culture is the problem of the heart. This is the attitude which fostered Japan's uniqueness all the way up to the Meiji period.

It was during the Meiji period that isolationism was abandoned and Japan opened its doors to the rest of the world for the first time. The subsequent days were a time of rapid introduction of advanced Western culture into Japan. The enthusiasm shown by the Japanese at this time was of exactly the same intensity as that of 1,300 years earlier, when they brought in all sorts of culture and learning from the advanced Tang culture. They spared no pains to introduce advanced Western culture in order to modernize Japan. The introduction of culture and civilization from other countries has continued actively, except during World War II, up to the present day.

A look at the culture of Japan today reveals that it is

雑多なものが入っています。フランスのものも、ドイツのものも、イタリアのものも、あらゆる文化が日本へ入っています。しかし、それが何となく日本化されてきています。このように今は各国とつき合っていますが、やはり江戸時代に他国とのつき合いがなく、中国の文化を根源として、それを日本独自のものに、知らず知らずに変えていったのと同じことが、鎖国時代ではないけれども現在行なわれています。

今私たち日本人の生活をみて、異様な感じはしませんけれども、よく注意してみると、それぞれの家にベッドがあり、畳の部屋があったり、日本古来の布団もあり、応接間にしても畳の敷いてある所もあり、それらのものが一つにとけあっています。椅子、テーブル、そして灰皿にしてもみんな外国から入ってきたものです。あらゆるものが入っていますが、それが何となく日本化されて、異国、他国のものが日本人の生活文化の中に入って不思議な形をしているという印象は、外国のどなたももたないであろうし、われわれ日本人ももっていません。

ですから、われわれ日本人、日本民族のある知恵、叡智、というものがあるとすれば、外国から入れたものをそんなに目立たない形において自分のものにしてしまうという才能があるのかもしれ

extremely varied. There are elements from France, from Germany, from Italy, and from all the other cultures of the world as well. But we have come to accept it all as having become Japanized. Thus, Japan associates with all the countries of the world today, but if we look closely, we find that the same process of converting everything we come into contact with into something uniquely Japanese, the process that went on during the long period of isolation after the introduction of Chinese culture, is still going on today almost without our being aware of it.

When we look at our life in Japan today, we feel nothing strange at first glance, but upon closer observation, we find a mixture of Western beds and furniture with the Japanese sleeping quilts called *futon*, and rooms with *tatami* mats on the floor next door to wood-floored rooms, and it is surprising to see that these all form a complete whole in our present-day lives. Our chairs, our tables, even our ashtrays were all imported from foreign cultures. All manner of things have come in, but all have been Japanized in some way or other. And perhaps the strangest part of it all is that neither we Japanese nor foreigners who visit us find it particularly remarkable that all these things have become very much a part of our daily life.

Thus, it can well be said that the greatest talent of the people of Japan is to take in things from other countries and subtly convert them into something that is very much their own. In this context, we find that the modernization of Japan

ません。そういう意味で、明治をスタートとした
近代化の時代は100年以上を経過した現在でも続い
ています。これからも続くでしょうが、日本が江
戸時代に作り上げた日本文化を失うことなしに、
明治以降は外国の文化をその上に入れています。
しかも目立たない形で日本化しています。新しい
日本の文化というものが現在作られつつあるし、
これからも作られていくであろうと思います。

　しかし、江戸から続いている、先ほど申し上げ
た文学でも絵画でも、たえず心を真中において、
心を描こうとしている。それは、失われることな
く、今私たちは受けついでいるし、そしてまた、
将来も受けつがれていくに違いないと思います。
ただ、いろいろな他国の文化がたくさん入ってい
ますから、それを吸収し、常に心を真中においた
文化は、いろいろな形に変化していくけれども、
その根源になる水脈は消えることなく続いていく
ことと思います。これが日本の文化の独自性だと
思います。

which began with the Meiji Restoration in 1868 has now been going on for more than one hundred years, and it is still continuing in full force. It will most likely continue on into the future, but we have managed at the same time to maintain and protect the unique Japanese culture that was created during the Edo period in the midst of the foreign cultural elements introduced since the Meiji Restoration. And we have quietly transformed all these new elements into something very Japanese. Thus, a new Japanese culture is also in the process of being formulated today, and I feel certain that this process will continue far into the future.

However, the attitude of centering everything around the expression of the heart in both literature and painting that I mentioned earlier has continued to prevail from ancient times, through the Edo period and on through all the modernization up to the present day. This is the legacy we artists of today have received from our forefathers, and I feel certain that it will continue to be a valuable inheritance for the Japanese artists of generations to come. Of course, along with the further introduction of elements from other cultures, and the absorption of those elements, our "heart-centered" culture will naturally undergo some alterations, but the basic approach will continue and never disappear. I believe that this is the unique character of the culture of Japan.

日本文化の選択原理
Principles of Selection in Japanese Culture

小松左京
Sakyō Komatsu

　　地図をご覧になると、おわかりと思いますが、日本という国は、アジアの東の端、大陸のすぐそばにある島国です。

　島国ではありますが、この国は大文明圏のあったユーラシア大陸とは、ごく近いわけで、朝鮮半島とは、北九州から約200キロの海峡を隔てて、相対しております。また、大陸中国との距離は、上海から九州西部の五島列島まで、およそ700キロ弱しかありません。しかも、ここには、日本海流、または黒潮と呼ばれる、非常に強い、北向きの海流がありまして、昔でも、船で3〜4日も航海すれば日本に来てしまう近さだったわけです。

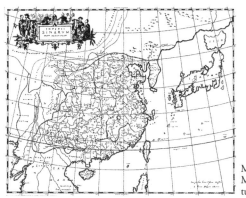

Map by Martino Martini (17th century)

A look at a world map will reveal that Japan is an island nation situated just off the east coast of the Asian continent.

While it is an island nation, it lies extremely close to the Eurasian continent with its great civilization. In fact, Japan is only two hundred kilometers from the Korean peninsula across a narrow strait, with the north part of its island of Kyūshū being the nearest to Korea. And Japan's closest point to the Chinese continent is located in the Gotō Islands off the western coast of the same island of Kyūshū. The distance between the Gotō Islands and Shanghai is less than seven hundred kilometers. In this same part of the sea we find the Japan Sea Current, along with the Black Current. The latter is a very strong northern-flowing current that made it possible for sailing ships to cross this distance in the short space of

そして、日本のすぐ西には、3500年前から、大きな文明を築き上げた、中国が控えており、また、日本海流の流れてくる方向には、インド文明が、東南アジアの方まで進出して来ておりました。この文明は、ヒンズー文明という形でも到来しましたし、また、仏教文明の格好でも来ていたのです。

　このような状況でしたから、アジアの大文明圏の、いろいろな文物というものが、歴史的に非常に古い時期から日本に入って来ているわけです。ところが、周辺諸国の場合と、日本とを比べてみますと、伝播してくる文明の、受容の仕方の上で、一つの大きな違いを見いだすことができます。

　普通、文明というものは、その基礎に一つの大きな原理があるもので、その原理に伴って、いろいろな社会システムや文化が出来上がっているわけです。日本もたしかに、ある時期、いわゆる部族国家から統一国家になる時に、このような文明原理の影響を受けております。

　日本の場合、一番強い影響を受けたのは、むろん中国文明です。たくさんのものを、日本は受け取りました。漢字などというものを入れておりますし、1300年ぐらい前ですが、中国で発達していた一つの社会政治制度で、律令制と呼ばれるものを入れております。それに伴って、儒教というものも入ってまいります。

three or four days even in ancient times, making Japan seem much closer to Shanghai than it actually is geographically.

Thus, we find that China, with its great civilization dating back 3,500 years, is situated just to the west of Japan. And in the direction of the flow of the Japan Sea Current, Indian civilization made inroads into southeast Asia very early. This civilization came in the form of both Hindu and Buddhist culture.

Under these conditions, we find that cultural artifacts and elements from greater Asian culture found their way to Japan in very ancient times. However, when we compare the case of the other surrounding island nations with that of Japan, we find a distinct difference between their acceptance of these cultural elements and that of Japan.

Normally there is some large principle behind a civilization, and the various social and cultural systems of that civilization are based upon that principle. Even in Japan, it is clear that at the time of the transformation from a tribal nation to a unified nation, the influence of such a cultural principle was in evidence.

In the case of Japan, it was naturally Chinese civilization that exerted the greatest influence. Many things were introduced to Japan from China. The Chinese characters known in Japan as *kanji* were introduced about 1,300 years ago, and a sociopolitical system known as the *ritsuryō* system which had been developed in China was adopted. Along with this system, Confucianism was brought to Japan as well.

ところが、日本は、そのような文明的に進んだ諸物を入れながら、そのシステムのすべてを受容するのではなく、日本側の選択によって、その一部または全部を落としてしまうことがあるのです。

　たとえば、日本は、7世紀から8世紀にかけて、中国周辺の、アジア文明圏の国々と同じように、律令制度というものを入れて、一生懸命に、律令国家を創り上げるわけです。ところが、その律令制度の中で、日本人自身もあまり気がついていないことなのですが、かなり重要なシステムが、二つほど落ちてしまっています。

　一つは、宦官（かんがん）の制度であり、他の一つは、科挙——つまり地方の秀才を試験によって選抜して中央へ集め、役人にするという制度です。

　律令制度が入ってきますと、日本の天皇は、ハーレムをもたなければならなくなります。後宮に、皇后は1人ですが、妃を何人、夫人を何人という具合に、女性をもたなければならないわけです。これは律令の制度によって、皇帝には、必ず血のつながった世継ぎを作らなければならなかったためで、そのための一つの保険として、ハーレムを作って、たくさんの淑女を入れたのです。

　この制度は、日本の、天皇を中心とした律令制の中にも導入されまして、『源氏物語』をお読みになるとおわかりのように、そこには華やかな、

But at the same time that Japan accepted these advanced cultural elements, it did not adopt the systems exactly as they existed in their original form in China. Rather, through a peculiar system of selectivity, the Japanese adopted the elements they desired and ignored all others.

For instance, like the other Asian nations around China, Japan adopted the *ritsuryō* system mentioned above and made intense efforts to develop into a *ritsuryō*-oriented nation during the seventh and eighth centuries. But even though most Japanese people were not aware of it, in their adoption of the *ritsuryō* system there were two important elements that were completely dropped.

One of these was the eunuch system, and the other was the classical examinations for government service in which brilliant young men from the provinces came to the capital to compete for appointments.

As a result of the adoption of the *ritsuryō* system, the Emperor of Japan was required to have a harem. Only one of his wives held the title of Empress, but he had a number of other wives as well. This was required as a sort of insurance policy to make sure that the Emperor would have a direct heir to the throne.

The effect of this system in Japan is brilliantly expressed in the intrigue and romance of the novel titled *The Tale of Genji*.

宮廷の、後宮ロマンスも発生しております。

　ところで、一般的には、ハーレムを管理するのは、律令制では、去勢された男性である宦官です。しかし日本の場合、ハーレムの制度を入れているにもかかわらず、宦官というものを作っておりません。宦官の制度は、アジア全域に、わりと広く存在しておりまして、もちろん、朝鮮の律令時代には存在していましたし、インド、ペルシャ、オスマントルコなどにもあったわけです。その宦官のシステムが、日本の律令制からは、すっぽりと落ちてしまっております。

　また面白いことに、宦官だけでなく、この制度の背景になる、一つの大きな牧畜技術としての、家畜の去勢というものも、日本には入ってきておりません。これは、有史以前から、日本でも家畜が飼われていたことを考えますと、実は、おどろくべきことでありまして、こちらの方が、宦官制度の欠落よりも重要かもしれません。

　有史以前から家畜が飼われていたと申しましたが、歴史時代に入りますと、牛馬を、かなりの規模で飼っていたことは、さまざまな記録から明らかです。たとえば、中世の「さむらい」たち、つまり武家軍団は何千という騎馬の利用によって高速移動が可能だったのです。かなりの数の馬が、組織的に飼われていたのは、これによっても証明

Generally speaking, under the *ritsuryō* system as it operated in other nations, the harem was managed by men who had been castrated, known as eunuchs. But while the imperial harem system was introduced into Japan, the system of eunuchs was not. The eunuch system existed throughout most of Asia. It was, of course, utilized during the Korean *ritsuryō* period, as well as in India, Persia, and Ottoman Turkey. But it was completely left out of Japan's *ritsuryō* system.

It is interesting to note that not only was the eunuch system for humans left out of Japan's *ritsuryō* system, but the custom of castrating animals, an important livestock technology that formulated the background for the human one, was not utilized in Japan either. When considered in light of the fact that Japan had raised livestock since the beginning of recorded history, it is quite surprising that the custom of castration was never used, and this may be an even more important point for consideration than the dropping of the eunuch system.

There are clear records that show that cattle and horses were raised in great numbers in Japan since ancient times. For instance, we find that during the middle ages, the military men known as *samurai* used thousands of horses in cavalry forces that were capable of moving at great speeds. This is proof positive that quite a large number of horses were raised in an organized manner. And cattle were also, of course,

されます。牛も、もちろん同様の規模で飼われていました。しかし、これだけ家畜を飼っていながら、遊牧社会の最大の家畜コントロールの技術ともいえる、去勢技術というものを、実は、日本人は、20世紀のはじめまで知らなかったのです。

20世紀のはじめ、中国で、義和団の乱というものがありまして、歴史ではこれを北清事変と呼んでおります。そこで、日本の将兵も、北京駐留の他の7ヵ国（アメリカ、イギリス、フランス、ドイツ、イタリア、オーストリア、ロシア）の在外武官たちと一緒に、55日間、北京の公使館区域に籠城するわけです。

その時、日本の軍馬は小さいのに非常に気が荒いのに対して、西洋のアラブ系の馬は、馬格が立派で、堂々としているのに、実におとなしく、いうことを聞くことに気づき、この時はじめて、日本人は、去勢という技術があることを知ったという話があります。

まあいわば、日本人は、そのくらいのんきな家畜文化をもっていたともいえるでしょう。しかし、文化の伝播という点からみますと、この、去勢技術を入れなかったという事実は、ちょうど、車があり、馬がいたのに、馬車、戦車が日本には出現しなかった、ということとも、おそらく関連しているように思われます。

もちろん、この背景には、日本の地形も関連しているでしょう。日本には山地が多く馬車、戦車

raised and kept on a similar scale. But while livestock was raised on this large scale, the major livestock control technique of the nomadic races—castration—was not known in Japan until the beginning of the twentieth century.

At the beginning of the twentieth century, the Boxer Rebellion broke out in China. Historically, this is known as the Northern China Affair. At that time, Japanese soldiers were confined within the Peking embassy area along with those from seven other nations—America, England, France, Germany, Italy, Austria, and Russia—for fifty-five days.

The story is told that the Japanese noticed that in contrast to the small size and rough nature of their war horses, the Occidental Arabic horses were noble and grand in appearance and extremely docile. As a result of this, the Japanese learned of the technique of castration in horse-breeding for the first time.

It could, of course, be said that this is evidence of how careless Japanese breeding techniques were up to that time. However, viewed from the standpoint of cultural transmission, the fact that castration had not been adopted in Japan appears to have been related to the fact that horse-drawn carriages and battle wagons never appeared in Japan either.

Of course, this must be considered against the background of Japan's topography. Japan has vast mountainous

を有効に使用できる広大な場所、及び広い道路が
なかったということもありましょうが、それだけ
では、馬車がまったく使われなかった理由は説明
しきれません。ともかく、日本では、馬車文明と
いうものは、明治になるまで入ってこなかったの
です。

　このような、外来文物の導入に際して、選択作
用が見られる例は、他にもいろいろあります。

　日本では、ある時期、儒教の影響を非常に強く
受けまして、親孝行であるとか、それに類する、
儒教型の道徳というものは、かなり入ってきてお
ります。しかし、儒教の根本原則の一つである、
同姓不婚という制度は、日本に入ってまいりませ
んでした。同姓不婚というのは、同じファミリー
ネームをもつ男女は、結婚できない。また、異な
った姓の男女が結婚しても、お互い、もとの家の
姓を名乗るという制度です。

　日本では、中国文明が入ってくる以前から、婚
姻については、かなりのんきな制度をとっており
まして、たとえば大和朝（7世紀以前）の天皇家
ですと、いとこどうしの結婚は、しょっちゅうあ
ります。また、母が違うと、父が同じでも、兄妹
での結婚は別に問題とはされませんでした。一度
だけ、同じ母から生まれた皇族の兄妹が恋におち
いりまして、この場合は、罪に問われております。
このような話はいろいろあっても、同姓不婚とい

areas where horse-drawn carriages and battle wagons would not be of much use, and is sadly lacking in broad flat plains and wide roads. But this cannot serve as the entire reason for the total absence of the horse-drawn carriage. In any case, the horse-drawn carriage civilization did not come to Japan until after the Meiji Restoration in 1868.

There are any number of other examples where this same system of selectivity is found at work in the introduction of cultural aspects from other nations to Japan.

During one period in Japan's history, Confucianism exerted a strong influence in terms of filial piety and many other aspects of moral conduct. But at the same time, one of the most basic principles—that of banning the marriage of persons with the same family name—was not brought to Japan. Under this system, a man and woman of the same family name could not marry, nor did the woman change her family name when she married—both retained the family name of their parents throughout their lives.

Before the introduction of Chinese civilization, the marriage system in Japan was undefined. For instance, during the Yamato dynasty before the seventh century, there were many marriages between cousins in the Imperial Family. Even half-brothers and sisters were allowed to marry. There is only a single recorded case among the aristocracy of a brother and sister of the same mother falling in love and being punished for it. In any case, while there were special cases such as this one, the system of prohibiting marriage between

う制度は、入ってまいりませんでした。

　その他にも、たとえば、仏教文化が入ってきても、中世（12世紀頃～17世紀）になりますと、僧侶の妻帯肉食が許されるというような、ある意味では、のんきな仏教になってしまうということもあります。

　こうしてみますと、日本という国が、いろいろな、海外で発達した文物を入れる場合、『これは入れるけれども、これは入れない』という、一種の選択原理があるように思われます。システムのほとんどを入れるけれども、かんじんの部分を、いくつか落とす、という場合もあります。

　この、外来文明の、ある部分を落としてしまうくせ、というものが、日本文化の、ある意味では、ネガティブなものではありますが、非常に大きな特徴になっているという気がいたします。

　実は、文明というものは、単に、便利に発達した制度文物というだけではなしに、前にも申しましたように、たいていの場合、その奥に大きな原理、原則があります。

　たとえば、西洋文明の根幹の一つである、キリスト教文明の中には、人間というものはどういうもので、人間の生きる道は、こういうことでなければならず、世界・宇宙の秩序は、神のもとに、こうなっている、という原理が確立しております。同じように、仏教にも、イスラム教にも、中国の儒教にも、それぞれ異なった大原理があります。

persons of the same family name was never adopted in Japan.

Also, even with the introduction of Buddhist culture during the middle ages from the twelfth to the seventeenth century, priests were allowed to marry and to eat meat, resulting in a rather loose type of Buddhism in Japan.

Thus, we find that while this nation of Japan introduced quite a number of cultural elements from other countries into its own culture, this was done on the basis of a certain principle of selectivity: "We want this, but we don't need that." Most of a system would be introduced, but sometimes important parts would be left out entirely.

This habit of dropping aspects of imported foreign culture is a rather negative element in Japanese culture, but I feel that it is important.

In actual fact, civilization is not merely a set of systems developed for the sake of convenience, but rather, as I mentioned earlier, in the majority of cases there are deep-seated principles behind each cultural element.

For instance, in Christianity, which is one of the foundation stones of Western civilization, a number of basic principles have been established which determine the way people should live, and an ideal order for the world and the universe under the rule of God. In the same manner, there are great basic principles in Buddhism, in Islam, and in China's Confucianism as well.

しかし、このような異なる原理どうしが全面的に衝突した場合、そこには、さまざまな規模での、対立、征服、時には生死をかけた闘争などが、くり返し発生しております。文明というものは、たしかに、人間の生活を豊かにし、便利にし、世界を広くするものですが、現在までの諸文明の底には、その原理から外れるものは、一切排除するという傾向があることを否定できません。

　ところが日本は、幸か不幸か、島国だったために、外来文明による圧倒的侵略、征服というものを経験したことがなく、文明を主体的に入れることができ、入れる時に、それまでの日本人の、ごく自然に形成されてきた感覚と合わないものは、上手に外してしまう、という余裕があったように思われます。

　一つのパターンとして説明するとすれば、日本という国は、ある時期、国を開いて、一生懸命に、いろいろな文物を導入いたします。そしてしばらくすると、不消化状態におちいり、世の中がノイローゼ症状を呈してきます。今日の言葉でいうと、アイデンティティ・クライシスとなるわけです。

　そういたしますと、日本は、国を閉じまして、それで何百年かかけて、じっくりと、導入したものを消化するという余裕をもてた国だと思います。

When these deep-rooted principles came into direct confrontation with each other, struggles took place that ended in submission or even in battles to the death. Civilization does indeed enrich our lives, makes life more convenient, and broadens our perspective, but it cannot be denied that even today there are basic elements in each culture that reject ideas in conflict with themselves.

Because Japan is an island nation, it has never experienced invasion or defeat at the hands of a foreign culture. For this reason, Japan has always been able to introduce foreign cultural elements in a subjective manner, and has skillfully succeeded in eliminating anything that did not fit the sensitivities of its people in a natural manner.

To elaborate on one of the patterns that appears in this process: at certain times, Japan opened its doors to foreign culture and made concerted efforts to take in elements and objects from various cultures. Then after a certain amount of time passed, Japan would reach a point of saturation and the entire society would go into a state of cultural nervous prostration. In other words, it would face what we call today an "identity crisis."

Then Japan would once more close its doors and spend several hundred years digesting what it had taken in during the open-arms period, Japanizing the things it had accepted. Japan has always enjoyed this sort of cultural latitude.

ですから、日本文化というものは、外から見ると、ごちゃまぜで、いわゆるシンクレティズムというか、実に不思議なものになっております。「一体全体、国を統一している根本原理は何なのか」と外国の人々に聞かれることがありますが、聞かれてみると、私ども日本人も、「確かに、いいところだけ、つまみ食いしているな」という気になるのです。

　しかし、一人の日本人として、世界を見わたしてみますと、もう、人類社会全体が、かつての大文明の亡霊、たとえばイデオロギーとか、ファンダメンタリズムというような原理絶対主義から、卒業してもよい時期なのではないかという気がいたします。

　時にはヒューマニズムというものも、イデオロギーになってしまう場合もありますし、民主主義というものですら、民主的な運営方式というものから、民主「主義」という一つの原理が確立してしまいますと、これも大変攻撃的なものになってしまうことがあるように思われます。

　完全ではあるけれども、排他的な原理を、文明の基礎としておりますと、より広い地域を統合してゆく上で、熱狂的に、お互いをつぶし合うという、不幸な、へたをすると今日では、人類の滅亡につながるような事態を招くことになるのは、歴史が証明しております。

　日本が先どりしたという言い方はしたくありま

Thus, viewed from outside, Japanese culture has become a very strange mixture or syncretism of disparate elements. People from foreign countries often exclaim, "Are there no basic principles that unify this nation of Japan?" To which we Japanese can only reply that it would seem we have indeed only sampled here and there with no basic principle to rule our choices.

But, as a Japanese, when I look out at the rest of the world I cannot help but feel that it is about time for human society to rid itself of the ideological ghosts of the great late civilizations, such as fundamentalism.

There are even times when humanism becomes an ideology, and it seems that when we are dealing with democracy, once its principles are established, it has a tendency to become a rather aggressive "ism."

When a basic principle of exclusion becomes the foundation of a civilization, in an attempt to unify mankind on a broader scale it waxes so fanatical that it becomes destructive to other similarly-oriented civilizations. In the present we are faced with historical proof that this could eventually result in the total annihilation of the human race.

I do not wish to take the stand that Japan is ahead of the

せんが、いずれ人類社会全体が、こうした文化衝突を避けて、それぞれのよいところをとり入れていくような、いわばおだやかな文化交流によって、かつての原理主義から徐々に抜けてゆくのではないか、そしていずれは、新しい調和と統合の時代に向かうのではないか、そうあってほしいと思います。

rest of the world in this context, but I do feel that human society will in the future enter into a peaceful exchange of culture, wherein confrontations and collisions are avoided by the mutual acceptance of good points while gradually moving away from the "basic principle-ism" of the past. If this is achieved, our world will be able to move toward a new age of harmony and unification. And I sincerely hope that this will happen.

国際社会の中の日本文化

Japanese Culture within International Society

中根千枝

Chie Nakane

日本とか日本人、日本文化というものが、外国人からはなかなかとらえにくいとよくいわれます。いったい、日本とは何なのだろうかと。

　日本文化というと、まずお茶や生花とか、歌舞伎などがよくあげられたりします。一方現代のコンピュータやロボットがよく知られています。歌舞伎やお茶やお花が一方にあり、他方、性能のいい自動車とか、世界一の生産高を誇るロボットなどという二つの全く異なる性質のものによって代表されやすい日本文化なるものは、たしかに外国人にとって、たいへん理解しにくいものでしょう。

　そうなると、日本人が説明を求められることになります。ところが、日本の文化や日本の社会に

Many maintain that Japan, the people of Japan, and Japanese culture are quite difficult for foreigners to understand. So let us begin by trying to figure out just what Japan is.

When we speak of Japanese culture, we are normally thinking about such things as the tea ceremony, *ikebana*, or kabuki. We could also be referring to computers or robots in present-day terms. Thus, while we have the traditional arts of kabuki, tea ceremony, and *ikebana* on the one hand, we have the technological achievements of world records in the production of highly efficient cars and robots and so forth on the other. This dichotomy in Japanese culture may well be difficult to grasp for people from foreign countries.

For this reason, foreigners often demand explanations of Japan and the Japanese. Unfortunately, it is far from easy for

ついて説明するのは、日本人にとっても容易では
ありません。

　日本はアジアの一角にあります。そこで、西洋
の人にはむずかしいとしても、アジアの人々にと
っては、日本を理解することはむずかしくはない
だろうと思われるかも知れません。そうでもない
のです。洋の東西を問わず、日本は、たいへん理
解されにくい存在です。なぜ、そんなに理解され
にくいのか。その理由を、ここで考えてみたいと
思います。

　わかりにくい対象というものは、その実態が複
雑である場合が多いのですが、日本の場合、その
構成は決して複雑ではありません。むしろ、単純
すぎるからわかりにくいといえるかもしれませ
ん。たとえば、アメリカなどは、人種・民族の違
う人々、つまり、伝統的な習慣が大変異なる人々
が共存し、複雑な社会を構成しています。中国や
インドなどはその長い歴史をとおして、複雑な民
族、言語集団に属する人々から構成される社会と
して存在してきました。こうした複雑さは、日本
にはまったくありません。おどろくほどホモジニ
アス（同質的）な人口によって構成されているの
が日本です。

　歴史をさかのぼってみましょう。縄文時代、い
わゆる先史時代から、日本列島には縄文文化とい
う共通の文化がすでにありました。古い時代には、
アイヌとか蝦夷といわれる人々が日本列島に住ん

Japanese people to give clear explanations of Japanese culture and society.

Japan is located in one corner of Asia. Thus, many may feel that while Japan may be difficult for Westerners to understand, it must be easily comprehensible to the other peoples of Asia. But this is not the case. Japan is difficult to understand for people regardless of East and West. Just why is Japan so very difficult to understand? I would like to present my thoughts upon the subject here.

One of the reasons often given for the difficulty of understanding is its complexity. But there is nothing particularly complicated about the composition of Japan. It might be that it is the excessive simplicity of Japan that makes it difficult to understand. For instance, America is a complicated society made up of people from many different races and cultures, all with traditional customs that stand in strong contrast to one another. In other countries with a long history, such as China and India, the population is made up of groups of people who speak many different languages. There are no complications of this kind in Japan, for Japan's population is amazingly homogeneous.

Let us take a look back into history. In the prehistoric period, the Japanese islands were covered by a single cultural type known as Jōmon culture. There were also minority groups of people known as Ainu and Ezo. But they have

でいました。しかし、彼らも早くから混血が非常
に進んでしまっています。ですから、全体として
見ると、一つの民族が日本列島に長い間住んでい
たといえるでしょう。

　大陸の影響を受けて稲作が始まったのですが、
その稲作文化も、たちまち日本列島全体をおおっ
て、水田耕作に立脚した文化が日本全土に及んだ
わけです。

　ヨーロッパ、アジアの国々を見まわしても、衣
食住のどれをとっても、こんなに共通の文化をも
つ人々によって構成されている国は、ほとんどあ
りません。日本はまれにみるホモジニアス（同質
的）な社会なのです。こういうことからすれば、
実は案外理解しやすいのかも知れません。

　日本への理解をむずかしくさせているものに、
日本文化の性質にかかわるものがあります。日本
人、あるいは日本文化は、エクスプレッシヴ、つ
まり外に向かって自分をはっきり説明する、とい
うよりは、パッシヴ＝受身の文化なのです。何と
もいわない相手を外から見てわかりにくいのは当
たり前です。

　歴史的、文化的に見ても、パッシヴであるのが、
よくわかります。古くから日本は、大陸、とくに
中国からの文化の影響を強く受けました。近代に
入ってからは、西欧文化をどんどん吸収しました。
受容能力はきわめて高いものがあります。しかし、
中国から文化を受けたからといって、日本の一部

mixed extensively with the majority of Japanese. Thus considered from the broader view, only a single ethnic group has occupied Japan for a very long time.

Later, rice growing was initiated under the influence of the Asian continent. The rice-planting culture quickly spread throughout Japan, resulting in the creation of a national culture based on wet-paddy cultivation.

Looking at the various other nations of the world, both in Europe and Asia, it is hard to find another nation in which the entire population is included in such a common culture. In other words, Japan is an unusually homogeneous society. If Japan is approached from this point of view, it may be surprisingly easy to understand.

What seems to make Japanese culture difficult to understand is its nature. The Japanese people and Japanese culture have more of a passive than an expressive nature, an unwillingness to explain private things clearly. It is only natural that this makes it difficult for one viewing them from the outside to comprehend.

It is easy to see that Japan has always been both historically and culturally passive. Since ancient times, Japan has been strongly influenced by the culture of the Asian continent, particularly China. And in modern times, Western culture has been introduced and absorbed at a dazzling pace. Japan has an extremely high level of receptivity. But the

が中国式になったり、西洋の文化のせいで西洋と同じようなものが日本にできるわけではありません。中国文化や西洋文化をいつも日本化してしまうのが特色です。その意味で日本的な母体の強さは、相当のものといえましょう。

　たとえば、儒教をとりあげてみますと、日本人が儒教として認識しているものは、本国の中国のそれとはずいぶん違います。身近な例を一つあげましょう。儒教精神にのっとると、「身体髪膚これを父母に受く」といって親への孝というのは、もう絶対的なものです。ところが、日本では、孝について儒教の影響をうけて同じような表現をしますが、日本人の本当の考え方は、「親に孝行しなければならぬ、なぜならば、親は自分を養育し育ててくれたからだ」ということができます。中国人は、親は自分の現在あるもと、悪い親であれ、育ててくれなかった親であれ、親は親、だから孝行しなければならぬと考えるのです。こういうふうに、日本の儒教的考え方は、本家のそれとは、すこし違ってきています。

　西欧に源をもつ近代教育とか近代企業のあり方もここ日本では、西欧のそれとはずいぶん違っています。うわべは西洋と同じに見えても、ちょっと深く入ると違ってくるのです。ですから、西洋人には、よけいわかりにくくなるわけです。西洋人から見ると技術面、工業化の面では、欧米に勝るとも劣らない近代化をしているのに、日本人、

assimilation of Chinese and Western culture has in no way made Japan anything at all like China or the West. Japan has a unique history of always Japanizing Chinese and Western culture. In this context, it appears as though the strength of Japan's cultural base is quite formidable.

For instance, let us take a look at Confucianism. What Japan thinks of as Confucianism is quite different from what it is in China, the country of its origin. Let us consider a concrete example. In the context of Confucian thought, everything we have was received from our parents, and therefore fidelity to parents is an absolute condition. However, in Japan, this concept has developed as fidelity to parents in return for the nurture and care received from those parents while growing to adulthood. But in China, since the parent is one's source, whether the parent is evil, whether that parent raised one or not, it is believed that a parent is a parent, and for this reason alone fidelity to parents is demanded. In this way, the Confucian ideas have been modified in Japan from their source in China.

Japanese modern educational and enterprise systems find their source in the West, but they are quite different in practice in Japan from their Western counterparts. While they may appear the same as the West on the surface, even a slightly deeper look will reveal the differences. This is what makes Japan even more difficult for Westerners to understand. From the viewpoint of Westerners, Japan is comparable with

日本社会は、やはりエキゾチックだということになります。これは、どうしてだろうと探りだすと、またたいへんむずかしくなってきます。一つには、日本文化はさきにふれたパッシヴであることにも関連するのですが、きちんとした独自のフレームワーク、形とか骨組みがないことが指摘できます。反対に、そういうものがあまりに強いと、外国の文化を受容同化するのはむずかしいといえます。

同化能力が強いというのは、どういうことでしょうか。ひと言でいうならシチュエーショナル・アジャストメントに適している。つまり、いろいろな条件に対して、対応能力がきわめて秀れていることです。日本文化とは、同じ基盤を維持しながら、本体に弾力性をもたせ、その時その時に対応してゆく、可変性に富んだ文化であると思います。

私はある時、西洋とか中国、インドに比べて、日本は軟体動物のようなものであるといったことがあります。西洋などは、哺乳類、馬とかライオンのようなもの、骨格があってはっきりしています。日本は骨格のないナマコのような生物に似ているともいえましょう。原則がはっきりした形であらわれず、常に様相が変わるし、きまった形を持たない、だから、外から見ると大変わかりにくいということになるのです。

これは日本人の考え方にもよくあらわれています。これほどの長い歴史をもち、文化をもっている社会としてはたいへん珍しいことに、いわゆる

the West in terms of technological advances and industrialization, but Japanese people and Japanese society seem very exotic. An attempt to figure out the reasons for this can be an extremely complicated task. One reason, however, is that, related to the passivity mentioned earlier, Japanese culture has no clear and individual framework of its own. If there were such a strong framework here, it would likely be difficult to assimilate foreign cultures.

What is it that facilitates the assimilation of other cultures? In a word, it is the ability to respond to a large variety of conditions which might best be referred to as "situational adjustment." It seems that Japanese culture is elastic in its ability to meet and respond to different situations while maintaining its own solid foundation.

In comparing Japan with the West, China, and India, I once spoke of Japan as a mollusk. The West is like a mammal, such as a horse or a lion, with a clear skeletal structure, while it can be said that Japan is like a sea cucumber. Its basic principles take no clear form, meaning that it is always changing shape and has no rigid skeletal structure of its own. Thus, viewed from the outside, it is most difficult to understand in practical terms.

This is clearly in evidence even in the Japanese way of thinking. Japanese society is unusual in the fact that in spite of the great length of its history and its refined culture, it has

哲学を発達させたことはありません。中国やインドでは、世界から注目を浴びる思想家や哲学者が出て、その国、社会の文化を外国の人々にもわかるように表明した歴史があります。日本には、そういうものが全然といっていいほどありません。原則を明示して他に向かって説明するものがない。それでは日本には何もないのだろうか、いい加減にただ浮かんでいるだけだろうかといいますと、そうではありません。

日本人の行動様式は、原則にてらして行動するのではなくて、何か中にもっていて、それがさまざまなものにぶつかった時の対応にあらわれてくるわけで、一定の性向＝トレンドをもっています。それが、日本の文化のありようといえると思います。

なぜ、こうなのでしょうか。日本の社会は、きわめてホモジニアス＝同質的ですので、ある意味で、社会的、文化的にまとまりがいい。ですから、はっきりした原則をうちたてて、みんな、これでいこうなんていわなくてすみます。つまり、原則は必要ないというわけです。

たとえば、中国の場合、いろいろな民族がいるし、言語の違う人もたくさんいます。そこでは、常に原則を提示し、全体を統合してゆくことが必要です。インドにしても同じことがいえます。そういう意味で、日本社会とか日本文化を考えるとき単に西欧と対比するだけでなく、中国やインド

developed no philosophy *per se*. Both China and India have produced philosophers who have attracted the attention of the world, and both of these countries have produced great thinkers that speak for their society and culture. But in Japan there is nothing of this type to speak of. Japan has no basic philosophical principles that can be explained with clarity. Does this mean that Japan has no code of thought, that it is just floating somewhere in ethical space? No, this is not the case.

The Japanese style of behavior is seen not in action in accordance with basic principles, but rather in terms of inclinations or trends that appear when something people have deep inside themselves comes up against a situation that requires some sort of reaction. And I think that this is the way Japanese culture works.

Why are the Japanese this way? Since Japanese society is so homogeneous, in a certain sense it has a strong social and cultural coherence. Thus, it is not necessary to establish a set of basic principles by which everyone agrees to act. In other words, basic principles are not necessary.

For instance, in the case of China, there are a number of different peoples, many of whom speak different languages. In such a situation, it becomes necessary to maintain a set of basic principles as the ideal in order to unify the nation effectively. The same set of circumstances exists in India as well. When Japanese society or culture is considered in this con-

と対比すると、違いがわかってくると思います。要するに、日本の文化は、きわめて同質な人々、同質な文化をもつ人口の中から発達したシステムであるといえます。

日本文化について、その特色があらわれた面であえてとらえてみますと、次のような特色が指摘できます。一つは、仕事に関してスピード感を重要視することです。スピードに加えて正確さも大事にされます。たとえば、国鉄のダイヤ、あるいはNHKや民放のTV・ラジオ番組が1秒の狂いもなく行なわれてゆく、こんな国は、世界中どこにもありません。こういう正確さ、精密さとスピード、いわゆるピシッピシッという感じが得意な文化です。

もう一つ、それに加えてフィニッシング・アップ（仕上げ）の水準が高く、出来上がりがきれいでなくてはいけないということです。日本の現代技術なども、こういうプレサイズネス、スピード、フィニッシング・アップのよさなどが貢献しているのではないかと思います。

それから、社会の、自分を取りまく人々の中での秩序を常に守るのも特徴の一つです。日本人が何人か集まって、お話でもしようかということになると、たちまち、誰が一番上、次は誰というふうにさっと席次が決まります。こういう社会のオーダーを常に自然に保てるということも、諸社会

text, the differences become clear in comparison not only with the West but also with China and India. In other words, Japanese culture can be said to have developed as a viable system for a homogeneous population with an equally homogeneous cultural outlook.

One might venture to say that one of the unique features of Japanese culture is the importance placed upon a sense of speed in work. Along with speed, precision is also considered important. For instance, the timetables for the national railways and the program schedules for both NHK and commercial TV and radio are carried out without a single second's discrepancy. There is no other country in the world that demands such punctuality in these areas. Japanese culture takes particular pride in this sort of precision, accuracy, and speed.

Another work element where high standards are maintained is the thorough and complete finishing-up of any job one may turn one's hand to. I feel that Japanese technological accomplishments have been made thanks to these elements of precision, speed, and thoroughness.

Another special feature is the constant maintenance of discipline in one's dealings with those of one's own social circle. When Japanese people gather together to talk about something or other, the first thing they do is decide upon the pecking order of the individual members of the group. Japan is far out front among the various societies of the world

のなかで群をぬいています。個人の自由とか、個人の意思の表明ということよりも、自分を取りまく集団の中に、自分を適切に位置づけることを優先します。それは、日本人が、常に集団あるいは社会的環境を前提として個人の社会生活を営み、ものを考えているしるしでもあります。

こういうあまり類例のない社会なので、外国の人々に理解してもらうのは、たしかにむずかしいでしょう。けれども、少しずつでも理解してもらわなければなりません。そのためには、日本人側の努力も必要です。いい面ばかりを知らせるのではなく、困っている面も知らせる。外から見るとこう見えるけれども、中ではこうなんだ、そういったことを、外国の人々に知らせていく必要があるでしょう。そうして、少しずつでも、日本に対する理解を深めてもらいたいものです。

Sea cucumber

in the constant natural maintenance of this sort of social order. More than the freedom of the individual, or the right of the individual to express his own opinions, the Japanese give top precedence to finding the proper position within the group of which they are a part. This, of course, derives from the fact that Japanese people always give the group or the social environment precedence in their daily life.

As Japan is a unique society in these ways, it certainly does seem a difficult matter to gain the understanding of people from foreign countries. But we must work little by little toward this goal. For this purpose, the effort of the Japanese people themselves is also necessary. We must not concentrate all our efforts upon showing our good points to others. Rather, we must show them the things that trouble us as well, and explain that while we may appear one way when viewed from the outside, the actual situation is something quite different. We must work to let other people know the truth about us. I hope that even little by little other peoples will deepen their understanding of Japan.

英語で話す「日本の文化」
Japan as I See It

1997年 9 月19日　第 1 刷発行
2000年 9 月22日　第 6 刷発行

編　集　　NHK国際局文化プロジェクト
　　　　　講談社インターナショナル株式会社

翻　訳　　ダン・ケニー

発行者　　野間佐和子

発行所　　講談社インターナショナル株式会社
　　　　　〒112-8652　東京都文京区音羽 1-17-14
　　　　　電話：03-3944-6493（編集部）
　　　　　　　　03-3944-6492（業務部・営業部）

印刷所　　大日本印刷株式会社

製本所　　大日本印刷株式会社

講談社バイリンガル・ブックス

英語で読んでも面白い！

- 楽しく読めて自然に英語が身に付く日英対訳表記
- 実用から娯楽まで読者の興味に応える多彩なテーマ
- 重要単語、表現法が一目で分かる段落対応レイアウト

46判変型 (113 x 188 mm) 仮製

講談社バイリンガル・ブックス　（オン・カセット/オンCD）英語で聞いても面白い！

[cassette] 印のタイトルは、英文テキスト部分を録音したカセット・テープが、また [CD] 印のタイトルは英文テキスト部分を録音したCDが発売されています。本との併用により聞く力・話す力を高め、実用的な英語が身につく格好のリスニング教材です。